ITALIAN TRIVIA

by

Nicholas J. Falco

Quinlan Press
Boston

Published by Quinlan Press
131 Beverly Street
Boston, MA 02114

Library of Congress
Catalog Card Number 86-60595
ISBN 0-933341-46-6

Printed in the United States of America
July 1986

Open my heart and you will see
Graved inside of it, "Italy."

Robert Browning

Acknowledgements

Thanks to:

Sandy Bielawa, for a fine job of editing;

Mary McCaffery, for initiating this project and structuring the book;

Roberta Bohlert, for typing the manuscript; and

Robert Astarita and Angelina Pellegrini, dear relatives who made all of this possible.

In memory of our parents and relatives, and to all the countless Italian immigrants who cherish their Italian heritage yet are proud to be Americans.

Yeh! That's us!!

Happy Holidays —

Pat + Dick

Jess + Damon

Contents

Lump the whole thing! Say that the Creator made Italy from designs by Michael Angelo.

Mark Twain

Tutti Italiano

1. What was Christopher Columbus's grandfather's name?

2. Who was the foundress of the Ursuline order of nuns?

3. What member of the elite Carabinieri police of Italy has been proposed for sainthood?

4. What does the "Alfa" in Alfa Romeo stand for?

5. What disease particularly affects people of Mediterranean background—especially Italians?

6. The Bulgari name is renowned in Italy and in many other parts of the world for its association with fine jewelry. The founder of the company was Sotirio Bulgari, who came to Italy in 1879. Name the country from which he emigrated.

7. In 1814 this man became the first commanding officer of the oldest branch of the Italian army. Who is he?

8. What is Italy's second largest city in population?

9. How many universities does the city of Milan contain?

10. What town in South Carolina is named after a famous Italian resort on the Adriatic Sea?

11. In what year did Giuseppe Garibaldi, Italian patriot and general, die?

12. What country sponsored John Cabot's (Giovanni Caboto's) expeditions along America's eastern seaboard in the late fifteenth and early sixteenth centuries?

13. In 1955 a bronze bust of Felice Pedroni was erected in his honor on the campus of the University of Alaska. What did Pedroni do?

14. Name the place of birth and death of Fr.

Charles Pise, editor, educator, historian, and author of the first Catholic novel in the U.S.

15. Name the Roman general who defeated Hannibal in the Second Punic War.

16. What does the Italian word *belvedere* mean?

17. Where are the islands of Capri and Ischia?

18. Where are the islands of Asinara, La Maddalena and Caprera?

19. Where are the cities of Nuoro and Sassari?

20. Where and when was Marchese Guglielmo Marconi, the inventor of the radio, born?

21. Who was the prime minister of Italy at the close of World War I?

22. What was the original name of the cluster of islands that later became the City of Venice?

23. How many popes have had the name Pius?

24. Who discovered the magnetic rotating field?

25. What was the occupation of the father of the painter Giotto?

26. What was the occupation of Mussolini's father?

27. On October 15, 1985, the first video-conference between the United States and this Italian city was held to promote trade. Name the city.

28. What is the address of the International Association for Sicilian Monuments?

29. Name the church near Messina where the International Association for Sicilian Monuments established a museum, in 1985.

30. When did the Italian government legalize divorce?

31. What does the term *contadini* refer to?

32. What did President John Quincy Adams, historian William Prescott, and writer Nathaniel Hawthorne all have in common?

33. What is "Avventurina"?

34. Who was Saint Benedict's twin sister?

35. Who was Toscanelli?

36. What five guidelines did the Romans use to govern themselves?

37. The *Nina,* the *Pinta* and the *Santa Maria* were Christopher Columbus's ships during his historic 1492 voyage. Which was his flagship?

38. For whom was the Castel Nuovo in Naples built?

39. From what area in Italy had Napoleon's family originally come?

40. Who was Silvio Pellico?

41. Name the three political figures who masterminded the revolutionary events leading to the unification of Italy in 1861.

42. Nicolo and Nicola both are Italian for Nicholas. Why the difference?

43. In 1548 the Jesuit Order opened its very first school for boys. In what city?

44. The Jesuit Order's famous plan for running schools is called the *Ratio Studiorum.* The final draft of this document was drawn up in 1599. Who was the author?

45. If you say "thank you" to an Italian, what will he or she answer?

46. What was the chief magistrate called in the former republics of Venice and Genoa?

47. What was the section of southern Italy from Sicily to Naples settled by the ancient Greeks called?

48. Name the conical stone dwellings found in parts of Apulia.

49. Who is considered the first outstanding microscopist?

50. In 1985, at the conclusion of the first Congress of Religious Choirs held at the Vatican on the occasion of the European Year of Music, the world's largest choir sang. How many were in this choir?

51. Who were the three Italian dignitaries awarded honorary degrees by Fordham University in the 1950s?

52. According to the 1980 Census, what percentage of the population of the states of Alaska and Hawaii is of Italian extraction?

53. Approximately when was the Roman Coliseum built?

54. Name the Papal representative who spoke at the United Nations 40th anniversary celebration in October 1985.

55. Who founded the Italian youth movement Comunione e Liberazione (Communion and Liberty)?

56. Who was the first European to describe the splendor of Niagara Falls?

57. What contribution did the German

geographer Waldseemuller make to America?

58. Did the Apostle Paul ever preach in Italy?

59. In what city did the "italic" type style originate?

60. A millinery shop is a hat shop. The word is derived from what Italian city?

61. After whom did Mother Frances Cabrini name the first hospital she founded, in New York City in 1892?

62. When was the Bank of Italy, later to become the Bank of America, opened?

63. In what year was atomic physicist Enrico Fermi born?

64. In what year did Enrico Fermi win the Nobel Prize?

65. In his lifetime, Enrico Caruso received eleven decorations from six different countries. Can you name the countries?

66. Mario Andretti, considered by many to be the best race car driver in the world, said that he was inspired as a young man by

another great Italian racer. Can you name him?

67. Where was jockey Eddie Arcaro born?

68. When and where did Giulia Buitoni start out in the macaroni business?

69. When Italian music lovers shout, "Ancora!" what are they demanding?

70. Name the pope who created the first Catholic diocese in the United States.

71. Who is the patron saint of television?

72. Dell'Api, Apicella, Apione, Lapini and Laponi are Italian last names deriving from the name of what industrious insect?

73. What was eighteenth-century Italian Cesare Beccaria interested in?

74. Who was the first European to hold a university chair in economics?

75. Who was Pauline Borghese?

76. On what date was Italy proclaimed a kingdom?

77. What was the last name of Pope Leo XIII?

78. What did the Italian people decide in a referendum held on June 2, 1946?

79. Name the Roman leader who in 49 B.C. crossed the Rubicon River.

80. What is the legendary date of the founding of Rome?

81. How high is Mount Etna in Sicily?

82. The largest lake in Italy, though not the most popular with tourists, is ______ .

83. The famous Castel Sant' Angelo was originally built as a mausoleum to Emperor ______________________ .

84. The writings of ______________, an ancient Roman statesman, greatly influenced and helped develop the concept of a society founded on liberty.

85. In what century were Dandolo, Ghisi, Foscolo and Barozzi the leading merchants in Venice?

86. *Suum cuique tribuere* was the definition of justice formulated by Roman jurists. The phrase later became a basic concept of Western law. What does it mean?

87. The shroud believed to be the one in which Christ was buried is preserved in what city?

88. Name the year in which the Council of Trent first convened.

89. What animal did the Carthaginian conqueror Hannibal use to help transport some of his materials across the Alps?

90. Where was the late stigmatist Padre Pio born?

91. In what city is Dante buried?

92. What denomination was the first-class postage stamp which depicted the Verrazano Bridge?

93. In what section of Queens, New York did Padre Pio's father live? What was his occupation?

94. What saint is honored at the oldest Sicilian feast in the United States, and where is it held?

95. What was the population of Italy as of 1983?

96. Geographically, Italy is the approximate size of what state?

97. Who lived in exile for two years on an Italian isle off Sardinia?

98. How many square miles is the Italian island of Malta?

99. Who succeeded Peter, the first pope?

100. The Ponte Vecchio is located in what city?

101. What river runs through Florence?

102. What saint's life is depicted on the doors of the Bapistery in Florence?

103. The obelisk in front of the Church of Santa Maria Novella was used for a ____________ for a time.

104. What scientific principle did Galileo test from the Tower of Pisa?

105. What four countries border on Italy?

106. *Frutta di stagione* is Italian for what?

107. Name the Italian city known for its famous marble quarries.

108. Into what fountain in Rome would you toss a coin in order to insure your return?

109. What was the first church in Italy dedicated to the Virgin Mary?

110. Who is the patron saint of beekeepers?

111. Name the country after which some famous steps in Rome are named.

112. What cathedral was built by Constantine in the fourth century?

113. Highways are called what in Italy?

114. ____________ is a lesser known buried city than Pompeii, but nearby and equally historic.

115. What modern city is built on the ruins of this buried city?

116. The acronym of which organization also means "farewell?"

117. Who founded the Franciscan order of nuns?

118. What is the affectionate name given to St. Francis of Assisi in Italy?

119. Who is acknowledged as the greatest of all band organ makers?

120. Are there more or less than one hundred Italian provinces and regions?

121. The ancient name for Wales, which is also a Sicilian family name, is ____________ .

122. Calabria is located in what part of Italy?

123. Who is the patron saint of Naples?

124. What is the free-standing belltower in Italian churches called?

125. What is the Italian term for "played slowly"?

126. What is a *chiesa?*

127. How many perfect games did champion bowler Andy Varipapa bowl?

128. Name the supermarket chain founded by an Italian-American family in Manhattan in the 1940s.

129. Name the developer of the Lionel model train.

130. When did Italian Franciscan priests first settle in New York State?

131. What was the name of the American political party of the 1850s with a program of keeping immigrants out of office?

132. What president issued an order to recruit musicians from Italy to organize the United States Marine Band, and from what area were they recruited?

133. Who were the two brothers who aided the future saint Elizabeth Seton, and from what province were they?

134. People of the town of Ferrara are called what?

135. When was the Communist Party of Italy founded?

136. In what year was Cicero born?

137. What great Italian city was virtually destroyed by an earthquake in 1909?

138. In 1952 who became world heavyweight boxing champion?

139. In what year was the ancient city of Pompeii destroyed?

140. In what year were Sacco and Vanzetti executed?

141. What famous oceanliner sank off the American coast in 1956?

142. Name the two Italians who introduced printing to the New World in the sixteenth century.

143. What was the family name of Pope Paul VI?

144. What famous football coach was born on June 11, 1913?

145. What famous monastery was virtually destroyed near the end of World War II?

146. What Renaissance genius died on May 2, 1519?

147. When did the explorer Giovanni Verrazzano sail into what was to become New York Bay?

148. In what year was Michelangelo born?

149. In what year did the Rizzoli Publishing Company first open a bookstore in the U.S.?

150. In 1901 Giuseppe Verdi died at the age of 88—in what city?

151. When was Pope John XXIII born?

152. What is the maiden name of Mrs. Bob Hope, and when did the Hopes celebrate their golden anniversary?

153. During some Italian feasts, a large platform is carried consisting of a tall tower of wood or plaster on which is found a small band. What is this tower called, and what does it mean?

154. What was the name of the American woman whose cries for help went unheeded and whose murder became a metaphor for some New Yorkers' tendency to shut their eyes to trouble?

155. Where in Italy did the Ronzoni family, of macaroni fame, come?

156. His friends might call a boy with this name "Guy." What would his proper name be in Italy?

157. How many children did the late world-renowned tenor Giovanni Martinelli have?

158. Americans say, "He's fit as a fiddle." Italians say, "He's fit as a __________."

159. What does *miramar* refer to?

160. What did Thomas Jefferson call his home?

161. The volt is named after an Italian physicist. Who was he?

162. Who were the first to utilize fanfare, the playing of trumpets and drums to introduce an announcement of great importance?

163. "It is his simplicity and modesty which endears him almost as his courage . . . . His food was of the simplest; a little cold meat or salami, bread, cheese and chocolate. Often he shared his meal with the soldiers near him." These words were written of which World War I leader?

164. Where were the Etruscans from?

165. What famous bridge is depicted on the wrapping of gum sticks in Italy?

166. Name the husband-wife team who sailed into Brooklyn Harbor on July 18, 1985, to become the winner of the first Brooklyn Cup trans-Atlantic regatta.

167. In Italy, what name was given to the year 1985?

168. He was born Fernando de Bouillon in twelfth-century Portugal. Italians took him to their hearts and made him one of their favorite saints. Who was he?

169. In the United States a person is said to be as "good as gold," while in Italy he is said to be ______________________.

170. Where is the Mezzogiorno?

171. What tree is symbolic for an Italian's love of family, friends and mother nature?

172. "No duty is more urgent than that of returning thanks." What famous bishop of Milan—also a saint—is credited with this quotation?

173. What religious order has always been in charge of the Vatican radio station?

174. The "Jolly" is a very large hotel chain in Italy. Can you name another such chain?

175. What is the unlikely name of one of Italy's most famous mountain climbers?

176. Who is considered the father of the Italian language?

177. *Dio e il Popolo,* "God and the people," was a phrase used by what leader of Italian unification?

178. CIT is Italy's national tourist organization. For what do the letters stand, and when was the organization founded?

179. What is the airport in Rome called?

180. Who is the largest magazine and newspaper publisher in Italy?

181. Name the violently anti-Italian Massachusetts politician of the early twentieth century.

182. ______________ is the colloquial Italian word for "laborer." (The word incorporates a part of the body signifying how work is done.)

183. Via Veneto is sometimes called "Rome's Fifth Avenue." What street is Palermo's Fifth Avenue?

184. The Italian government hopes to build a bridge between the mainland and Sicily. If it does, it would be more than double the length of the Verrazano Bridge in New York City, the longest existing suspension bridge. How long would the Italian bridge be?

185. What is the angelicized version of the family name Pellegrino or Pellegrini?

186. "19 Via Morganini" is an address of a

typical street in Italy. Is there anything wrong with the way it's written?

187. What is intarsia?

188. Only one librarian—an Italian—was ever hung in effigy. Who was this man?

189. Who is credited with the invention of the compass?

190. Marco Polo, who traveled extensively in the Far East, was made governor of which Chinese province?

191. Maria Montessori (1870-1952) achieved world-wide recognition for her educational theories and methods. Is she known for anything else?

192. Try your luck at these! Name the telephone area codes for the following six Italian cities: Bergamo (2 digits), Campobasso (3 digits), Genova (2 digits), Messina (2 digits), Napoli (2 digits), and Roma (1 digit).

193. What is an *edicole sacra*?

194. To which eastern country was Pope John XXIII once an apostolic delegate?

195. "Ciao" means "goodbye" or ______ .

196. If an Italian wants to get your attention,

what is he or she likely to say?

197. How does an Italian bid a formal farewell?

198. When a Catholic Mass is offered *Pro Popolo,* for whom is it being offered?

199. For what is Cardinal Pavan known?

200. Who were the "Periti"?

201. What is the Italian game which resembles bowling?

202. What was the family name of Saint Pius X?

203. Fill in the missing word which was found in the opening sentence of the will of Saint Pius X: "I was born __________, I have lived __________, and I wish to die __________.

204. Name the Roman hotel that overlooks the famous Villa Borghese.

205. Before the terms B.C. and A.D. were created (sometime in the sixth century), A.U.C. was used. What does the acronym stand for?

206. Nineteenth-century English poets Elizabeth Barrett Browning and Robert Browning lived in Florence for a period. Name their home.

207. What is the significance of AB-57?

208. Name the two chemists who developed AB-57.

209. What is the fur coat worn by some Sardinian villagers called?

210. What is the name of the Sardinian item of clothing that resembles the Scottish kilt?

211. Translate the following Latin sentence, a significant one during the Christmas season: *"In illo tempore, exiit edictum a Caesare Augusto, ut describeretur universus orbis."*

212. What Italian saint is honored by Scandinavians, especially the Swedish?

213. Where is the Malpensa Airport?

214. What was the motto of the city of Williamsburg in the eighteenth century?

215. What was the name of the first mutual aid society, organized in Tampa, Florida?

216. Why was Rome, Georgia, so named?

217. Why were Saints Cosmas and Damian chosen as patron saints for the famous Medici Family of Florence?

218. Where was the fighter Rocky Graziano born?

219. When did Father Pio receive his stigmata?

220. Who was the 1967 Nobel Prize winner who came from Turin?

221. This comedian, who was born in the Bronx in 1925, actually wanted to become an operatic star. One of his best-known sketches concerned an astronaut and was first performed a few months before the U.S. sent our first astronaut into space. Name the comedian.

222. What is the highest award that Italy bestows on a non-resident?

223. When was the Schola Cantorum, a school in Rome for singers, first organized?

224. Where was the very first opera house built?

225. In what century was the Medical School of Salerno established?

226. In what century was the University of Bologna established?

227. In what century was the University of Padua formed?

228. What university did the Polish astronomer Copernicus attend?

229. Who was Piano Carpini?

230. "I can build any kind of public and private buildings, and can transport water from one place to another . . . ." These words were written in 1485 by what Italian genius?

231. When did Columbus arrive back in Spain after his discovery of the New World?

232. How many voyages did Columbus make to the New World?

233. Where was Galileo born?

234. Who invented nitroglycerin?

235. Who invented the internal-combustion engine?

236. In 1801 the astronomer Giuseppe Piazzi was director of the Palermo Observatory when he made what major discovery?

237. What did the astronomer Giovanni Schiaparelli, director of the Brera Observatory in Milan, do and discover?

238. In what year was the Italian Geographic Society founded?

239. Name the early nineteenth-century Italian explorer who made major excavations in Egypt.

240. Who was the pilot for Stephen Decatur during the war between the United States and the pirates from Tripoli?

241. When Mother Cabrini died in 1917, approximately how many nuns were Sisters of the Sacred Heart?

242. In what type of work were they engaged?

243. What was "The March on Rome"?

244. What are Nuraghi?

245. What was the "Sicilian Vespers"?

246. Is "Gheghe" a language, a food or a city?

247. What type of naval ship is the Italian *Giuseppe Garibaldi*?

248. What do Simonetta, Fontana, Veneziani and Pucci have in common?

249. What fairy tales would Italian children be reading if they read the following: *Cenerentola, Pollicino, Capuccetto Rosso, La Bella Addormentata* and *Giacomo e La Planta Di Fagioli*?

250. Where in Sicily are the best-preserved

Greek temples with Doric columns?

251. What was a Roman forum?

252. What is considered the best-preserved building of ancient Rome?

253. When did the eruption of Vesuvius, which buried the city of Pompeii, occur?

254. What was the topic discussed in Pius X's encyclical *Motu Proprio?*

255. When was it issued?

256. According to 1980 statistical data, where does Italy rank among European nations in the production of cement? Steel? Automobiles?

257. What does *pazienza* mean?

258. To whom does the term *fuorusciti* refer?

259. "The only thing I want is to be free; it is the only thing this fellow cannot give me." Who is "this fellow"?

260. Who was Giovanni Caproni?

261. Who founded the anti-Fascist Mazzini Society?

262. Who was the first president of the Mazzini Society?

263. ALITALIA, the airline, is also known as ________________ .

264. What is the Italian-American area of San Francisco called?

265. When was hockey star Phil Esposito born?

266. What was the last name of Pope Pius XII?

267. The internationally known singer Lily Pons was part Italian. What other nationality was she?

268. Who was called the "Workingman's Pope"?

269. Name the labor encyclical which won him that title.

270. What religious order did Mother Margerita Crispi found?

271. Name the Italian magician who performed in New York City during the early nineteenth century.

272. To what religion did Vito Volterra belong?

273. In what month in 1966 did devastating floods hit Florence?

274. Where were post office boxes first introduced?

275. With what American university was Father Michael Tomei, one of the earliest teachers of moral theology, associated?

276. Where is St. Nicholas buried?

277. Who were the founder and foundress of the religious order Daughters of Saint Paul?

278. What do Bargello, Uffizi, Pitti and San Marco have in common?

279. What do these share in common: Carmine, Apostoli, Orsanmichele and Santo Spirito?

280. What do these share in common: Baglioni, Continental, Augustus and Londra?

281. Name the road in Italy that is well known as one of the most scenic routes in the world

282. What is a *cameriere*?

283. What does an Italian say when he or she wants you to come in?

284. When you're finished eating at an

Italian restaurant, the waiter will hand you a *conto.* What is it?

285. What are the average maximum daily temperatures in Naples during May, June and July?

286. What is the average maximum daily temperature in Milan during December?

287. Where in Italy did Saint Francis tame a famous wolf?

288. What is a "water bus" in Venice called?

289. What are the four small islands in Lake Maggiore called?

290. Where is the seaport of Catania?

291. What is a *presepio?*

292. Trees which grow in Surrey and Buckinghampshire, England, may also be found in southern Italy on the __________ Peninsula.

293. What feast day is celebrated on December 31?

294. What does A.M.D.G. stand for?

295. What does A.R.M. stand for?

296. What astronomical invention was created by Father Angelo Secchi, S.J. (1818-1878)?

297. Where did Saint Bridget of Sweden die?

298. In what century did the architect and sculptor Brunelleschi live?

299. Which fourteenth-century saint was advisor to both church and public figures?

300. In what century was the Leaning Tower of Pisa built?

301. How many steps must one climb to reach the Tower terrace?

302. Which is the second largest island in the Mediterranean?

303. When was Aldo Moro of the Christian Democratic Party murdered?

304. Where did Nobel Prize-winning novelist Grazia Deledda come from?

305. Name the motion picture studio right outside of Rome that was once the scene of most Italian motion-picture productions.

306. What city in Italy is sometimes called "The Flemish City"?

307. How large is the Republic of San Marino?

308. What do Italians call Turin?

309. Approximately how many miles is it from Cortona to Florence?

310. What is the largest Gothic building in Italy?

311. What is the beach area of Venice called?

312. What city in northern Italy was once the chief port of the Austrian empire, around the turn of the twentieth century?

313. Where was the poet Horace born?

314. Is Sicily mostly mountainous or level?

315. ENIT are the initials of what organization?

316. What kind of coin is needed in a pay phone in Italy?

317. Give the Arabic number for this Roman numeral: MDCCCXCIX.

318. Where was Virgil born?

319. Who founded the famous Scuola Italiana de Cucina in New York City?

320. Who is credited with designing the first botanical garden?

321. Many regions of Italy have caricature mimics with which they have defined themselves for centuries. Can you tell with

what region each of the following characters are associated: Pulcinella, Pisquino, Gianduja, Meneghino, Zacometto, Stenterello?

322. Who designed the 1921 American Peace Dollar, which was minted between 1921 and 1935?

323. Who posed for Miss Liberty on this coin?

324. What is the title of Vatican City's newspaper?

325. Who are Babbo and Nonna? Compare and Commare?

326. What was the name of the American ship that received the first salute from a foreign government given to a ship carrying the American flag (November 16, 1776)?

327. What was the largest local in the United States?

328. In what area of Italy is the family name Astarita especially prevalent?

329. What is the name of Carroll O'Connor's Italian adopted son?

330. From what port in the late fourteenth and early fifteenth century did instructors leave for France to teach the French the art of lace making?

331. How many declensions does Latin have?

332. In what city was the first paper-making mill set up?

333. In what modern piazza in Rome stands the house where Saint Bridget of Sweden lived—and where she died in 1373?

334. Name the archaeologist who, through her perseverance and scholarly examinations, confirmed the exact location of the tomb of Saint Peter in 1968.

335. In 1945 Father Robert Biasiolli, O.M.I., performed a baptism in Greenland. What was its significance?

336. What was the name of the Franciscan monastery in Spain where Columbus stayed during the period he was seeking financial aid for his expedition?

337. In what Asiatic country did the missionary Robert De'Nobili plant the seeds of the Catholic faith?

338. Who was the first woman ever to receive a Ph.D.?

339. From which university?

340. There are six colors that share names with three cities and a province in Italy. What are they?

341. Who designed the uniform of the Swiss Guards?

342. What Italian-American national service organization has as its motto "Service Above Self"?

343. In 1985, who was elected president of this organization?

344. In what year was the American Italian Historical Association formed?

345. According to the old saying, what Italian city should one visit before dying?

346. When was the Congregation of Saint Charles, better known as the Scalabrini Fathers, founded?

347. Which of their order serves as the Director of the Italian Seamen's Club in New York City?

348. While president, Herbert Hoover appointed the late Edward Corsi to what post?

349. Where were jeans first manufactured?

Answers

1. Stephen Columbus—he was a merchant from Genoa.

2. St. Angela Merici—she founded the order in Brescia, Italy, in 1537.

3. Sergeant Salvo D'Acquisto, who was murdered by the Nazis in 1943 while saving twenty-two hostages.

4. Anonima Lombarda Fabbrica Automobili (Lombard Automobile Factory Inc.)

5. Cooley's Anemia

6. Greece—he came to Italy with just eighteen cents in his pocket.

7. General Thaon di Revel, first commanding officer of the Carabineri

8. Milan, with 1,580,000 according to the 1982 count. Rome is first with 2,834,000.

9. Five

10. Rimini

11. 1882

12. England

13. He founded Fairbanks, Alaska.

14. Born in Annapolis, Maryland, in 1801, Father Pise died in Brooklyn, New York, in 1866.

15. Scipio (the Elder)

16. "Fine view" or "beautiful view"—a belvedere is usually an open roofed gallery built in an upper story to provide a view of the scenery.

17. In the Bay of Naples

18. Off the coast of Sardinia

19. In Sardinia

20. In Bologna in 1874

21. Vittorio Orlando

22. Rialto

23. Twelve

24. Ferrari, in 1896

25. Shepherd

26. Blacksmith

27. Genoa

28. Piazza Farnese 51, Rome 00186

29. St. Onofrio in Casalvecchio, Siculo

30. This very controversial law was passed on December 1, 1970.

31. "Country people"—farmers or farm laborers

32. At one time or another, these great personalities all studied Italian.

33. A chocolate-brown opaque glass with gold flecks. It was popularly used in brooches, and a great deal of it was made in Venice.

34. Saint Scholastica

35. A mathematician, astronomer and

geographer who in 1474 stated that the shortest way to India was westward across the Atlantic, not along the African coasts

36. 1) *Pietas:* respect for elders, ancestors and religion. 2) *Continentia:* self-control. 3) *Aequitas:* equanimity and impartiality. 4) *Virtus:* manliness, or proper conduct becoming a man or soldier. 5) *Fides:* the obligation to be faithful to one's word.

37. The *Santa Maria*

38. Charles I, King of Sicily in the mid-thirteenth century

39. Tuscany

40. One of the principal fighters in the nineteenth-century struggle against Austrian rule in Italy

41. Camillo Cavour, Giuseppe Garibaldi and Giuseppe Mazzini

42. Men from the northern part of Italy usually end the name with an "o," while those from the south usually use an "a."

43. Messina, in Sicily

44. Claudio Acquaviva, fifth Provincial of the order

45. *"Prego"*

46. The doge

47. *Magna Graecia* or "Great Greece"

48. *Trulli*

49. Marcello Malpighi, a professor at the Universities of Pisa and Bologna who lived in the seventeenth century

50. Fifteen thousand joined together to sing selections by Perosi, Bach and Handel.

51. Premier Alcide de Gasperi (1951), Foreign Minister Gaetano Martino (1955) and Prime Minister Mario Scelba (1955)

52. 2.2 percent in Alaska and 1.4 percent in Hawaii

53. A.D. 80

54. Cardinal Agostino Casaroli, the Vatican's Secretary of State

55. Msgr. Luigi Giussani, in Milan, Italy, in 1954

56. Father Francesco Bressani in the early 1600s

57. He was the first to suggest naming the newly discovered land after the explorer Americo Vespucci.

58. Yes, in A.D. 61, a year after he had been

shipwrecked off Malta. He was martyred in Rome probably in the year 67.

59. Venice

60. Milan

61. Columbus

62. The bank officially opened for business on October 17, 1904, in San Francisco.

63. 1901, in Rome

64. 1938

65. Italy (three), Germany (two), Spain (one), Belgium (one), England (two) and France (two)

66. Alberto Ascari

67. In Cincinnati in 1916

68. In the small town of San Sepolcro, Italy, in 1827

69. They are asking the performer or performers for an encore.

70. On April 6, 1789, Pope Pius VI created the Diocese of Baltimore.

71. Saint Clare of Assisi

72. The bee (*ape*)

73. Prison reform

74. The Neapolitan Antonio Genovesi, in 1754 at the University of Naples

75. The sister of Napoleon who was married to the governor of Piedmont

76. March 17, 1861—Rome became the capital ten days later.

77. Pecci

78. Italy would become a republic, which prompted King Humbert II to go into exile.

79. Julius Caesar, as an act of revolt against Pompey

80. 753 B.C.

81. 10,705 feet

82. Lake Garda

83. Hadrian

84. Cicero

85. The thirteenth century

86. "To give each his due"

87. Turin

88. 1545

89. The elephant

90. In the small town of Pietreclina in the province of Benevento on May 25, 1887

91. Ravenna

92. Five cents

93. Jamaica—he worked for the Long Island Railroad laying down tracks.

94. The Blessed Virgin Mary, under the title of Our Lady of Trapani; the feast is held in the Bushwick section of Brooklyn, New York.

95. 56,833,000

96. Arizona

97. Napoleon I, on the island of Elba

98. 122

99. Linus

100. Florence

101. The Arno

102. St. John the Baptist's

103. horse-race turnpost

104. Gravity

105. France, Austria, Yugoslavia and Switzerland

106. Fresh fruit

107. Carrara

108. Trevi Fountain

109. The Basilica of St. Mary Major (Santa Maria Maggiore)

110. Saint Ambrose

111. Spain

112. The Basilica of St. John Latern

113. Autostradas

114. Herculaneum

115. Resina

116. The Congress of Italian-American Organizations (CIAO)

117. St. Clare of Assisi

118. Il Poverello

119. Ludovic Gavioli of Modena, Italy

120. Less—there are ninety-one, including three in Sardinia.

121. Cambria

122. The south

123. Saint Gennaro

124. The campanile

125. *Adagio*

126. A church

127. Seventy-eight

128. D'Agostino's

129. Mario Caruso

130. 1855

131. The Know-Nothing party

132. President Thomas Jefferson; Sicily

133. Antonio and Filippo Filicchi of Perugia

134. Ferrarese

135. January 21, 1921

136. 106 B.C.

137. Messina

138. Rocky Marciano

139. A.D. 79

140. 1927

141. *Andrea Doria*

142. Giovanni Paoli and Antonio Riccardo, in Mexico and Peru, respectively

143. Giovanni Battista Montini

144. Vince Lombardi

145. The Benedictine Monastery at Monte Cassino

146. Leonardo da Vinci

147. April 17, 1524

148. A.D. 1475

149. 1964, on New York City's Fifth Avenue

150. Milan

151. 1881

152. Dolores DeFina; 1984

153. A *giglio,* which means "lily"

154. Kitty Genovese

155. San Fruttuoso, near Genoa

156. Gaetano

157. Three—Bettina, Antonio and Giovanna

158. fish *(Sano come un pesce)*

159. A seaview

160. Monticello, or "little mountain"

161. Alessandro Volta (1745-1827)

162. The ancient Romans

163. King Vittorio Emanuele, when he was at the Italian front fighting the Austrians

164. Tuscany

165. The Brooklyn Bridge

166. Pierre and Paola Sicouri, who set sail from Italy on June 16, 1985

167. "The Year of the Etruscans"

168. St. Anthony of Padua

169. *"buono come il pane"*—as good as bread

170. Southern Italy

171. The fig tree

172. St. Ambrose

173. The Jesuits

174. CIGA

175. Reinhold Messner

176. Dante Alighieri

177. Giuseppe Mazzini

178. Compagnia Italiana Turismo, founded in 1927

179. Leonardo da Vinci International Airport

180. The Rizzoli Editore Co. of Milan

181. Henry Cabot Lodge, who served as senator from 1893 to 1924

182. *Braccianti,* which is derived from the word *braccia,* meaning arms

183. Via Macqueda

184. 10,800 feet long, more than double the 4,260 feet of the Verrazano Bridge

185. Pilgrim

186. Yes, in Italy the number of the house is always written at the end of the street. Thus: Via Morganini 19.

187. Decorative or pictorial wood inlay—in Italy, some of the best examples are found in Sorrento.

188. Sir Anthony "Prince of Librarians" Panizzi. He was an outspoken critic against the Austrian occupation of Italy in the nineteenth century. He fled to England in 1823, became a naturalized citizen, and was appointed principal librarian of the British Museum.

189. Flavio Gioia, who lived in the province of Campania

190. For three years he was governor of Yangchow.

191. She was one of the first women in Italy to become a physician.

192. Bergamo is 35, Campobasso is 874, Genova is 10, Messina is 90, Napoli is 81 and Roma is 6.

193. A name commonly given to the sacred niches or little roadside shrines which dot many streets in Italian cities.

194. Turkey

195. "hello"

196. "Senta!"

197. "Arrivederci"

198. For the people; that is, for no one specific intention, but for all.

199. The Declaration on Religious Liberty issued by Vatican II—his scholarly writings together with those of the late Father John Courtney Murray formed the basis for this document.

200. The theological experts who attended Vatican Council II and who acted in the capacity of counsellors to the bishops

201. Bocce—15 points wins a game, 18 points in team bocce.

202. Sarto

203. poor

204. The Hotel Parco Dei Principi

205. *Anno urbis conditae,* "from the founding of the city"—Rome

206. Casa Guidi

207. This is the name given to the chemical product used to clean the Michelangelo frescoes.

208. Paolo and Laura Mora, of the Istituto Centrale del Restauro

209. *Mastrucca*

210. Raga

211. "At that time, an edict went out from Caesar Augustus that the whole world be enrolled." This sentence is from the gospel of St. Luke which begins the Christmas story of Mary and Joseph returning to Bethlehem to be enrolled in the Roman census.

212. Santa Lucia, St. Lucy, who was born in Sicily

213. Milan

214. *Virtute et Labore Florent Respublicae*—States flourish by virtue and toil.

215. L'Unione Italiana

216. Like Rome, Italy, the city in Georgia is built upon seven hills.

217. These third-century saints were physicians, and the name *Medici* means physician or doctor.

218. In New York City in 1922

219. September 20, 1918

220. Salvador Luria, who was honored for helping to "set the solid foundation on which modern molecular biology rests"

221. Charlie Manna

222. The Award of Commander of the Order of Merit of the Republic of Italy

223. The fifth century

224. In Venice, in 1637

225. The ninth

226. The eleventh

227. The thirteenth

228. The University of Padua

229. An envoy of Pope Innocent IV who was sent to China in 1245 to meet with the great Kahn. He was known as Father John.

230. Leonardo da Vinci

231. March 15, 1493

232. Four

233. Pisa

234. Antonio Sobrero, in 1846

235. A priest, Eugenio Barsanti, and Felice Matteucci, in 1852

236. The first asteroid, Ceres. It is also the largest, at 480 miles in diameter.

237. He discovered and measured the rotations of Mercury and Venus.

238. 1867

239. Giovanni Battista Belzoni

240. Salvatore Catalano, from Syracuse, Italy

241. Fifteen hundred

242. Staffing orphanages, nurseries, hospitals and schools

243. The Fascists' forceful seizure of power in Italy on October 28, 1922

244. Pre-Roman tower structures built in Sardinia

245. The revolt of the Sicilians against their French rulers on Easter Monday, 1282

246. It's a very ancient language spoken by some decendants of Albanians who settled in Sicily.

247. An aircraft carrier

248. They are fashionable clothing designers.

249. *Cinderella, Tom Thumb, Little Red Riding Hood, Sleeping Beauty,* and *Jack and the Beanstalk*

250. Paestum

251. The forum was a social and political hub of a city, a meeting place and market.

252. The Pantheon, built around A.D. 120

253. A.D. 79

254. Liturgical music

255. 1903

256. First, second and third, respectively

257. "Patience"—it is a common expression in Italy.

258. To those who fled Italy when Mussolini came to power

259. Mussolini. These words were spoken by Carlo Sforza, the Italian foreign minister, when he left the country at Mussolini's rise to power.

260. The designer of a WWI Italian fighter plane

261. Gaetano Salvemini

262. Journalist Max Ascoli

263. Linee Aeree Italiane

264. North Beach

265. February 20, 1942

266. Pacelli

267. French

268. Pope Leo XIII

269. *Rerum Novarum*, issued in 1891

270. Sisters Oblate to Divine Love, in the first half of the twentieth century

271. Signor Falconi

272. Jewish—he was one of a few outstanding non-Catholic scholars invited by Pope Pius XI to join the Papal Academy.

273. November

274. Albano, Italy, in 1820

275. Fordham University

276. Bari

277. Father James Alberione and Sister Thecla Merlo

278. They are all museums in Florence.

279. They are all churches in Florence.

280. They are all hotels in Florence.

281. The Amalfi Drive, which runs between Naples and Sorrento

282. A waiter

283. *"Avanti."*

284. The bill

285. 72°, 79° and 84°, respectively

286. 43°

287. Gubbio

288. A *vaporetto*

289. The Borromean Islands

290. Sicily

291. The Christmas manger

292. Gargano

293. The Feast of Sylvester I, a fourth-century Pope

294. *Ad Majorem Dei Gloriam,* that is, "For the Greater Glory of God"

295. *Alma Redemptoris Mater,* that is, "Loving Mother of the Redeemer"

296. The meteorograph

297. In Rome, in 1373

298. The fifteenth

299. Saint Catherine of Siena

300. The twelfth

301. 294

302. Sardinia

303. 1978

304. Sardinia

305. Cinecitta

306. Bologna

307. Twenty-three square miles

308. "The Little Paris"

309. Sixty-three

310. The Cathedral of Milan

311. The Lido

312. Trieste

313. Venosa, in southern Italy

314. Mountainous—at least two thirds of the island is nine hundred feet above sea level.

315. The Italian Government Tourist Office

316. A token called a *gettone*

317. 1899

318. Mantua

319. Mrs. Hedy Giusti-Lanham and Mr. Andrea Dodi

320. Professor Luca Ghini, a botanist and teacher. His gardens were in Pisa circa 1543.

321. Respectively: Naples, Rome, Piedmont, Milan, Venice, Tuscany

322. Anthony de Francisci of New York City, who also designed the discharge button issued to servicemen

323. His wife, Teresa

324. *L'Osservatore Romano*

325. Papa and Grandma; Godfather and Godmother

326. The *Andrew Doria*

327. Local 89, the Italian Dressmakers Union

328. In the town of Vico Equense and in some of the adjacent area near Naples

329. Ugo

330. Venice

331. Six

332. Fabrino, circa 1276

333. Piazza Farnese

334. Margherita Guarducci

335. Father Robert (1914-1980) was the first Catholic priest to administer this sacrament since the Middle Ages in this country.

336. La Rabida

337. India

338. A Venetian by the name of Lady Helen Lucretia Cornaro Piscopia, in 1678

339. The University of Padua

340. Raw Sienna and Burnt Sienna; Raw Umber and Burnt Umber, Venetian Red and Naples Yellow

341. Michelangelo

342. UNICO—Unity, Neighborliness, Integrity, Charity, Opportunity

343. Joseph L. Andreis

344. 1966

345. Naples—*"Primo vedi Napoli, poi muori"*

346. 1887

347. Father Joseph Cogo

348. Immigration Commissioner of Ellis Island

349. Genoa

Whether we regard the history of the Italian people or their contributions to letters, to science, and to the arts, or their zeal for progress in these modern days, they must be placed in the front rank of the world's great powers.

Nicholas Murray Butler, President of Columbia University (1923)

Statues, Sonnets, Cinema & Songs—The Arts

1. *Appocu appocu lus stissu timuri ci insigna a fari spinciri li mura: nascinu li cita ntra ddi chianuri da li mucchi di petri e crita dura. Lu scantu fu lu so legi laturi: contra la forza forma liggi e jura; e mentri d'autru carcera la fidi, s'incatina iddu stissu, e'un si nn'avvidi*
   Is the above stanza of poetry written in the Italian language?

2. How many square feet did Michelangelo paint on the Sistine Chapel ceiling?

3. Who is the patron saint of musicians?

4. Where in the United States is there a museum devoted to Garibaldi?

5. Who is credited with naming the notes on the musical scale?

6. Who painted the *Mona Lisa*?

7. Who wrote the epic poem *Orlando Furioso*?

8. If you see the word "*FINE*" in an Italian movie, what has just happened?

9. What is the connection between Chris Columbus and Sherlock Holmes?

10. Which Italian film director invented the "Spaghetti Western"?

11. What New England author wrote the 1940 novel *Deep Grow the Roots*?

12. Name the Italian journalist who in the early 1970s wrote the book *The Italians*?

13. What musical form is generally considered to mark the beginnings of Western music?

14. Name the artist noted for his sculpture of the meeting of Saint Francis and Saint Dominic.

15. Duccio's painting of Christ with two apostles is on display in the National Gallery in Washington, D.C. Which apostles?

16. What area in Italy did Duccio come from?

17. In what part of Italy has the marionette theater had its greatest development?

18. Professor Antonio Pasqualino was the creator of what mid-twentieth-century museum in Italy?

19. A marionette theater still flourishes in New York City's Little Italy. Name the family who runs it.

20. Name the classic silent movie of 1922 in which Rudolph Valentino plays the part of a Spanish bullfighter.

21. Which nineteenth-century French painter is famous for his full-length portrait of the violinist Paganini?

22. What was the religious background of the twentieth-century Italian artist Amedeo Modigliani? Where was he born?

23. Around 1917 Modigliani painted a picture of a woman emphasizing two different colors. Name the portrait.

24. One of the earliest novels to portray Italian-American life was written by Pietro Di Donato. What was it called?

25. Name the Italian-American architect who is considered the father of post-modernism.

26. *Monte Allegro,* by Jerre Mangione

(1909-), describes Sicilian immigrant life in what New York city?

27. *A Highly Ramified Tree*, by Robert Canzoneri, describes life in what two small villages?

28. Who created the fictional detective Ed Noon?

29. *The Blackboard Jungle,* published in 1954, was a book about urban schools. The author's pen name was ________. His real name was ________________.

30. Name the biographer who was a co-founder in the 1920s of the Leonardo da Vinci Art School in New York City.

31. Name the author, philosopher, lecturer and TV personality who in 1983 had four of his seven books on *The New York Times* Bestseller List.

32. Where and when was the poet and critic John Ciardi born?

33. Who won the Richard Rogers Award for the libretto of the Broadway musical *Nine*?

34. What is the real name of the producer, director and choreographer of the Broadway musicals *A Chorus Line* and *Dream Girls*?

35. Name three nineteenth-century, Italian-born ballerinas who performed successfully in America, helping to lay the foundation for the Americanization of ballet.

36. In what section of New York state was ballet star Edward Villella born?

37. How long did the great baritone Antonio Scotti sing at the New York Metropolitan?

38. How old was composer Giancarlo Menotti when he came to this country? From which music school did he graduate?

39. Name the composer who won a Pulitzer Prize in 1957.

40. Was there ever an Italian-American president of the Juilliard School of Music?

41. Who won the 1979 Grammy Award for Best Pop Instrumental Performance?

42. Name the bandleader who was famous for his New Year's Eve telecasts from Manhattan.

43. Name the Italian-American star of the award-winning TV show "M*A*S*H."

44. Who designed the Juilliard School of Music at Lincoln Center?

45. What is considered Caruso's most popular role?

46. Enrico Caruso was once invited to din-

ner by the German kaiser. What toast did the kaiser propose that evening?

47. What was the first opera Licia Albanese sang at the Metropolitan Opera?

48. Name the star of the 1961 Tony Award-winning Broadway play, *Carnival*.

49. Were any of the top stars Italian in the 1946 war-related film *A Bell for Adano*?

50. Name the Italian-American who was one of the six dancers who made up the original Robert Joffrey Ballet when the company was formed in 1953.

51. Who published *The Reporter* from 1949 to 1958, and where was he born?

52. Did Catherine Gloria Balotta ever appear in the television hit "The Mother-in-Laws," with Eve Arden?

53. Who wrote the hit song "I Got You Babe"?

54. What conductor/arranger was best known for his adaptations of classics written by such immortals as Rachmaninoff and Tchaikovsky?

55. Name the best-known opera of the composer Vincenzo Bellini (1801-1835).

56. Where does the action of Ponchielli's opera *La Gioconda* take place?

57. What inspired Tchaikovsky to write *Capriccio Italien?*

58. Amilcare Ponchielli's musical masterpiece *Dance of the Hours* was used as the background for a Walt Disney movie. Name the movie.

59. The old radio program "The Lone Ranger" used as its theme song the music of what nineteenth-century Italian composer?

60. What was the first Italian opera produced in the United States in Italian with Italian singers? How many performances were given?

61. What famous Italian city is depicted in many of Canaletto's (1697-1768) paintings?

62. Who wrote the great novel *I Promessi Sposi?*

63. Orazio Borgianni's famous painting of St. Charles Borromeo is on display in the Church of Santo Adriano in Rome. What charitable deed is the saint performing?

64. Who wrote *Cantico delle Creature?*

65. What was the title of the musical based on the life of the first Italian-American mayor of New York City?

66. What is singer Connie Stevens's real last name?

67. Joe Durso, the sportswriter and broadcaster, wrote a history of what baseball team?

68. What woman conductor received the 1985 Stokowski Award for best conductor?

69. Michelangelo's famous *David* is located in what city?

70. At what former restaurant in New York City are two columns brought over from Pompeii located?

71. Name two famous nineteenth-century opera singers who for a time lived in the Bronx, New York.

72. In what year did the first American performance of *I Pagliacci* take place?

73. How many operas did the well-known director of the Metropolitan Opera House Gatti-Casazza produce?

74. In what year did the immortal Arturo Toscanini make his debut at the

Metropolitan Opera House? What opera did he conduct?

75. On November 2, 1857, what Verdi opera had its debut in New York?

76. In what year was the violin virtuoso Nicola Paganini born?

77. What famous painting by Leonardo da Vinci was commissioned in 1497?

78. Who composed the opera *Cavalleria Rusticana?*

79. What was the name of the theater in Rome where the opera *Tosca* was first produced?

80. Name the priest who, before entering priesthood, had been the musical director of the International Royal Grand Opera Company.

81. Who wrote the popular song "Avalon"?

82. Who was the composer of "Stairway to the Stars," "Blue Serenade" and "I'll Never Be the Same"?

83. Who played Archie Bunker's Italian next-door neighbor in TV's "All in the Family"?

84. What was the late songwriter Harry Warren's real last name?

85. Who wrote the book *Blood of My Blood?*

86. This popular singer who started on the Arthur Godfrey show in the late 1940s, has the same name as a macaroni manufacturer. Name him.

87. What is comedian Pat Cooper's real name?

88. As a young man, what did Perry Como do for a living?

89. Perry Como was one of how many children, and when was he born?

90. In 1964 composer Norman Dello Joio won an Emmy Award for the background music for a television documentary about ______________________________ .

91. The Boston Symphony was the first American orchestra to tour the Soviet Union. Name the American composer of Italian descent whose music was performed on this 1956 tour.

92. Giuseppe Fagnani painted the portrait of what famous statesman in 1852?

93. One of the earliest relief sculptures depicting the landing of the Pilgrims was executed to hang in a government building in Washington, D.C. Who was the sculptor?

94. Name the Franciscan priest who in the late 1930s organized a fife, drum and bugle corps of 460 boys and girls.

95. Pietro Di Donato, who wrote the classic *Christ in Concrete,* also wrote a biography of what saint?

96. Paul Gallico, the author of the memorable stories *The Snow Goose* and *The Small Miracle,* also wrote a biography of what Yankee baseball immortal?

97. Some of Shakespeare's plays, such as *Romeo and Juliet,* are set in Italy. How many times did the immortal bard visit that country?

98. When and where was the opera star Licia Albanese born?

99. The late great showman Liberace was Italian on his father's side. What was he on his mother's side?

100. ____________________ is an Italian-American award-winning author famous for his children's books.

101. ________________ is a high-spirited dance from the south of Italy.

102. There is a famous statue of the composer Verdi on New York City's West Side.

Encircling the pedestal are four life-size figures representing the composer's most famous characters. Can you name them?

103. The well-known statue of Columbus in New York City's Columbus Circle was erected to commemorate what anniversary of his famous voyage?

104. A very famous statue was loaned to New York City for exhibit at the 1964-1965 World's Fair. Can you name it?

105. Name the poignant Italian film of the 1970s which told the story of the adjustments Italian immigrants seeking work in Switzerland had to make.

106. Ernest Hemingway lived in several places in Europe, including a lovely little island right outside of Venice. Name the island.

107. Were Dante and Boccaccio contemporaries?

108. For what publication is Giorgio Vasari (1511-1574) famous?

109. Name the American pianist—Swedish on his father's side, Italian on his mother's—who became the first American to win the International Chopin Piano Competition. The year was 1970, the place, Warsaw.

110. *Six Characters in Search of an Author* is the most popular and well-known play of Nobel Prize-winner ________________ .

111. Name the sixteenth-century Italian composer who wrote over one hundred masses and other religious compositions.

112. Name the Italian-born painter who was a pupil of and then an assistant to the painter John Singer Sargent.

113. What baseball player, active especially in the 1960s, wrote an autobiography called *Seeing It Through*?

114. What was the late Bobby Darin's real name?

115. Who wrote the modern opera *Triumph of St. Joan*?

116. Where and when was the tenor Mario Del Monaco born?

117. Can you give the real name of the late Johnny Desmond?

118. Did people applaud Alfred Capurro when he starred on Broadway in such musicals as *Oklahoma* and *Kiss Me Kate?*

119. Is Fabian the first or the last name of the famous singer?

120. At what time of the year would Italians sing the hymn "Gesu Bambino"?

121. Who composed this hymn?

122. Harry Simeone and Henry Onorati were two of the three composers who wrote a popular Christmas song in the 1950s called ________________________ .

123. Name the cinematographer for the movie *The Deerhunter,* which so masterfully portrayed the drama of Vietnam.

124. The great composer Offenbach wrote which opera about a famous Italian?

125. What does the term *arte povera* indicate?

126. Who founded this style of art?

127. He was the author of *The Path to the Nest of Spiders,* and *The Non-Existent Knight,* and was also a collector of Italian fables. Who is this man, one of Italy's finest novelists?

128. Each Christmas season the Metropolitan Museum of Art in New York City puts up a large display of eighteenth-century Neapolitan Christmas creches for the public to view. Name the woman who donated these rare items to the museum.

129. What unusual phenomenon is depicted in the upper portion of *The Adoration of the Magi* by Giotto?

130. Which nineteenth-century American

sculptor was called "America's Michelangelo"?

131. When did the great Italian artist Botticelli live?

132. To what religious order did the renowned painter Fra Angelico (1400-1455) belong?

133. The Telfair Museum in Savannah, Georgia, has five larger-than-life-size figures of artists standing at its entrance. Two of them are Italian. Name them.

134. Who directed the cleaning and restoring of the Sistine Chapel, which was begun in 1980?

135. When did Michelangelo begin and when did he complete decorating the Sistine Chapel?

136. What is the title of the newsletter issued by the Italian Folk Art Federation of America?

137. Who wrote *De Monarchia?*

138. What is its main thesis?

139. St. Mary's, the mother church of the Carolinas and now the cathedral in Charleston, South Carolina, was completely redecorated in 1894 with some

twenty-three oil paintings and frescoes. Name the Italian artist brought over from Rome for this purpose.

140. The operas *Norma* and *La Sonnambula* were written by whom?

141. The opera *Lucia di Lammermoor* was written by whom?

142. When and where was the famous coloratura soprano Amelita Galli-Curci born?

143. Where does most of the action of Giacomo Puccini's *Madame Butterfly* take place?

144. *Amelia Goes to the Ball* was written by what modern Italian-American composer?

145. Where was Verdi's *La Forza del Destino* first produced?

146. When was *La Forza del Destino* first performed in the United States?

147. What is the first aria, a very famous one, which is sung in the last act of *La Forza del Destino?*

148. On what French writer's work did Donizetti base his opera *Lucrezia Borgia?*

149. Who wrote the text of this opera?

150. Who wrote the lyrics for Verdi's opera *Il Trovatore?*

151. Who wrote the opera *William Tell?*

152. What is the setting for Mozart's opera *Cosi Fan Tutte?*

153. What is the opera house of Milan called?

154. In what year was it built?

155. Who designed it?

156. What is the opera house of Venice called?

157. In what year was it built and by whom?

158. What is the opera house of Rome called?

159. After whom is the opera house San Carlo, in Naples, named?

160. How did the opera house in Milan get its name?

161. In the mid-eighteenth century a huge tapestry designed by the Flemish artist Geraert Van Der Streecken was completed. What was the subject matter of the tapestry?

162. When was the Statue of Columbus in St. Petersburgh, Florida, erected?

163. What was the middle name of the Italian sculptor Giovanni Benzoni (1809-1873)?

164. Which Italian musician is honored by a statue in Fairmount Park, Philadelphia?

165. The Italian sculptor Giuseppe Ceracchi (1740-1801) created a marble bust of which American president?

166. An exquisitely beautiful painting depicting an aged Saint Joseph holding the Infant Jesus tenderly in his arms was painted by what seventeenth-century artist?

167. The sculpture *Orphans,* by Pietro Montana, was done in 1931 in what type of marble?

168. What type of marble was used for the sculpture *Children and Gazelle,* by Anthony De Francisci, in 1937?

169. Name the actor who in the 1960s played Dr. Ben Casey on television.

170. Where was the well-known choreographer and dancer Peter Gennaro born?

171. Name the movie depicting the life of fighter Rocky Graziano.

172. Who was Frank Paul Lo Vecchio? Here's a hint: he recorded "That's My Desire," which sold over two million copies.

173. Name another hit of his which has an animal in the title.

174. This famous actress made many movies in the 1930s. She starred with Frederic March in Cecil B. deMille's *The Sign of the Cross* in 1932. Who is she?

175. Why did the late Japanese artist Roka Hasegawa visit Italy in the early 1950s?

176. Who portrayed the immortal Caruso in the motion picture *The Great Caruso?*

177. From a motion picture director's viewpoint, what was important about the 1950s movie *That Midnight Kiss?*

178. Who was known as "The Poet Laureate of Arkansas"?

179. For his performance in what movie was the late Sal Mineo nominated for an Academy Award?

180. When was Liza Minnelli born?

181. Name the director of such films as *Gigi* and *Bells Are Ringing.*

182. Where was this director born?

183. Who wrote the 1966 book *The Verdicts Were Just,* about the WWII trials?

184. What role did Rosa Ponzelle play when she made her debut at New York's Metropolitan Opera with Enrico Caruso?

185. Who wrote the novel on which the movie *Three Coins in the Fountain* was based?

186. For what was this author primarily known?

187. Who is the father of the Surrealist school of art?

188. Who wrote and was able to get produced the first successful opera?

189. Who introduced opera to the Germanic lands?

190. Domenico Scarlatti was considered the best ______________ of his time.

191. The Cappella Sistina is a famous choir in Rome. In what city is the Cappella Marciana based?

192. Did actor Paul Sorvino ever sing opera?

193. What are the real names of the singing duo known as The Gaylords?

194. *"C'era una volta . . . Un re! — diranno subito i miei lettori. No, avete sbagliato. C'era una volta un pezzo di legno."*

The above sentences are the beginning of what delightful book?

195. How old was Adelina Patti when she made her debut at the Academy of Music

in 1859 in New York in *Lucia di Lammermoor?*

196. What were *La Sentinella, La Nuova Napoli, Il Popolo* and *Corriere di Rochester?*

197. How long did Ezio Pinza sing with the New York Metropolitan Opera Company?

198. What was the name of the quartet in which Frank Sinatra sang as a teenager?

199. Who was "Pasquale Passaguai"?

200. What do the following three authors have in common: Al Santoli, Philip Caputo and John DelVechio?

201. Who was the founder of the magazine *Messenger of the Sacred Heart?*

202. Name the birthplace of the most famous male flamenco star of modern times, José *Greco.*

203. When was Leonardo da Vinci commissioned to paint *The Last Supper?*

204. When did the San Francisco Opera Association give its first performance?

205. Who organized the group?

206. Name the Sicilian sculptor who carved the

monument to the explorer Verrazzano in New York City.

207. The Alamo in Texas has a twentieth-century monument which was dedicated in 1936 to the heroes of this famous battle. Name the sculptor who did this work.

208. Who is credited as "The Father of the Violin"?

209. Where is the small bronze statue of a wild boar called *Il Porcellino* located?

210. What two early Italian film directors helped inspire the Americans D. W. Griffith and Cecil B. DeMille with their epics?

211. What does the group I Giullari di Piazza do?

212. What American poet won the 1985 Giuseppe Ungaretti Award issued by the Accademia Internazionale di San Marco di Belle Arti, Letters e Scienze, in Naples?

213. What fifteenth-century artist is considered to have painted some of the most beautiful representations of the Madonna?

214. At the age of fourteen, the above artist was apprenticed to the great ________ .

215. "All Gaul is divided into three parts"— so begins what famous work?

216. *I Vitelloni* and *La Strada* were two of the earliest films of what great director?

217. In what years were they produced?

218. In recent years, the United States Post Office has issued Christmas stamps featuring the work of Italian masters. Whose paintings were represented in the years 1970, 1971, 1975, 1978, 1981 and 1985?

219. Who is credited with establishing Italian theater in San Francisco?

220. A character famous with early twentieth-century immigrants because of his comic portrayal of the difficulties of life in the United States was Farfariello. Who was the actor who portrayed this role?

221. When and where was Luciano Pavarotti born?

222. What was his mother's maiden name?

223. Whom did Luciano marry?

224. In what role did Luciano Pavarotti make his opera debut?

225. Name the 1981 MGM movie in which he starred.

226. *Orlando Furioso,* by Renaissance poet

Ludovico Ariosto, is centered around what themes?

227. What is Sofia Loren's real name?

228. What literary great wrote these travel books on Italy: *Twilight in Italy, Sea and Sardinia* and *Etruscan Places?*

229. *Old Calabria,* by Norman Douglas, was written in what decade?

230. Who inaugurated the first "Live from the Met" PBS telecast in 1977?

231. What was the title of the biography written about this opera singer?

232. These are the opening bars of what piece of music?

Answers

1. Not really—it is written in Sicilian. The above is from a lengthy work by the Sicilian poet Giovanni Meli (1740-1815), considered the most accomplished poet who ever wrote in Sicilian. Translated, it reads:

   As time went on, fear taught these men how to erect great walls around themselves. And so from heaps of stone and dried up clay great cities rose along those valleys and fear was a legislator unto them. It set up laws and rights against brute force, and while it chained the faith of other men, it put itself in chains quite unawares. (Translated by Gaetano Cipolla of St. John's University, New York, and published by ARBA SICULA)

2. 8,600 square feet

3. St. Cecilia

4. In Staten Island, New York—it is known as the Garibaldi-Meucci Museum.

5. Guido D'Arezzo, the choir master of a Benedictine monastery in Italy. He introduced re, mi, fa, sol and la in the eleventh century.

6. Leonardo da Vinci

7. Ludovico Ariosto, in the sixteenth century

8. The picture has ended.

9. It's elementary, my dear Watson—Hollywood screenwriter Chris Columbus wrote the script for the movie *Young Sherlock Holmes.*

10. Sergio Leone

11. Mari Tomasi (1907-1965), of Montpelier, Vermont

12. Luigi Barzini

13. The Gregorian chant, developed by Pope Saint Gregory I in the sixth century

14. Andrea della Robbia

15. Peter and Andrew

16. Siena

17. Sicily

18. The International Museum of Marionettes in Palermo

19. The Manteo family

20. *Blood and Sand*

21. Eugene Delacroix

22. Jewish; Leghorn, Italy

23. *Woman in Blue, Red Necklace*

24. *Christ in Concrete*

25. Robert Venturi

26. Rochester

27. Palazzo Adriana in Sicily and Standing Pine in Mississippi

28. Michael Angelo Avallone, Jr.

29. Evan Hunter; Salvatore Lombino

30. Francesca Vinciguerra, who wrote under the name Frances Winwar

31. Leo Buscaglia, Jr.

32. In Boston, in 1916

33. Mario Fratti (1927-)

34. Michael Bennett's real name is Di Figlia.

35. Maria Bonfanti (1845-1921), Rita Sangalli (1849-1909) and Giuseppina Morlacchi (1843-1886)

36. On Long Island, in 1936

37. From 1902 until his death in 1921

38. He was seventeen and almost immediately enrolled at the Curtis Institute of Music in Philadelphia, graduating in 1933.

39. Norman dello Joio

40. Yes—Peter Mennin, whose real name was Mennini

41. Chuck Mangione, for his "Children of Sanchez"

42. Guy Lombardo — and his Royal Canadians

43. Alan Alda

44. Pietro Belluschi

45. Canio in *I Pagliacci*

46. "To your servant Martino, and if I were not Emperor of Germany, I should like to be Martino." Caruso had at first refused the invitation since his servant Martino had not been invited. The emperor apologized for the oversight.

47. *Madame Butterfly*

48. Anna Maria Alberghetti

49. No, the two stars were John Hodiak and Gene Tierney. The late Italian character comedian Henry Armetta had a minor role.

50. Gerald Arpino (He is also a choreographer.)

51. Max Ascoli, who was born in Ferrara, Italy, in 1898

52. Yes, she was the co-star, but most people knew her as Kaye Ballard.

53. Sonny Bono

54. Carmen Cavallaro

55. *Norma*

56. Seventeenth-century Venice

57. A visit to Rome at carnival time in 1880

58. *Fantasia*

59. Gioacchino Rossini (1792-1868) and his *William Tell Overture*

60. *Il Barbiere di Siviglia (The Barber of Seville)* was first performed on November 29, 1825, at the Park Theater in New York City. Twenty-three performances were given.

61. Eighteenth-century Venice

62. Alessandro Manzoni (1785-1873)

63. Tending the sick: victims of a plague which struck Milan in 1576

64. St. Francis of Assisi

65. *Fiorello*

66. Megna

67. The New York Mets (1970)

68. Joann Falletta of New York City

69. Florence

70. Delmonico's, at 56 Beaver Street

71. Adelina and Carlotta Patti

72. 1893

73. 177

74. 1908; *Aida*

75. *Rigoletto*

76. 1782

77. *The Last Supper*

78. Pietro Mascagni

79. The Constanzi Theater

80. Father Leonard Pavone

81. Vincent Rose

82. Frank Signorelli. He also wrote "Anything" with Tommy Dorsey.

83. Vincent Gardenia

84. Guarana

85. Professor Richard Gambino

86. Julius LaRosa

87. Pasquale Caputo

88. He was a barber.

89. He was one of thirteen children, and he was born on May 18, 1912.

90. The Louvre

91. Composer Paul Creston, whose real name was Giuseppe Guttoveggio. He was also the church organist at the "actor's church," St. Malachy's, in New York City.

92. Henry Clay

93. Enrico Causici, a native of Verona, in 1825

94. Father Henry A. Borrelli. This was considered the largest musical unit in New England, and possibly the U.S., at that time.

95. Saint Mother Cabrini, *Immigrant Saint*

96. Lou Gehrig: *Pride of the Yankees*

97. Never

98. In 1913 in Bari

99. Polish

100. Valenti Angelo author of *Hill of Little*

Miracles and *Angelino and the Barefoot Saint*

101. The tarantella

102. Leonara of *La Forza del Destino,* Falstaff, Othello and Aida

103. The 400th anniversary—it was done by the Sicilian sculptor Gaetano Russo.

104. Michelangelo's beloved *Pieta*

105. *Bread and Chocolate*

106. Torcello, in a country inn called Locanda Cipriani

107. Not exactly. Dante lived from 1265 to 1321, while Boccaccio lived from 1313 to 1375. The latter was a contemporary of Petrarch, who lived from 1304 to 1374.

108. A multi-volume masterpiece, *Lives of the Artists,* which became the basis of Italian art history

109. Garrick Ohlsson, who was twenty-two at the time

110. Luigi Pirandello, a Sicilian

111. Giovanni Pierluigi Palestrina (1526-1594)

112. Joseph Coletti

113. Tony Conigliaro of the Boston Red Sox

114. Walden Robert Cassotto

115. Norman Dello Joio

116. He was born in Florence in 1915.

117. John Alfred de Simone

118. They sure did, only they knew him as Alfred Drake.

119. The first—his last name is Forte.

120. This popular hymn is sung during the Christmas season.

121. Pietro A. Yon, in 1919

122. "The Little Drummer Boy"

123. Michael Cimino

124. *Christopher Columbus*—not one of his most famous works

125. Art made from everyday materials

126. Germano Celant, in Italy in the 1960s

127. Italo Calvino (1923-1985)

128. Loretta Hines Howard donated them in 1964.

129. A comet, usually referred to as Halley's Comet

130. Hiram Powers

131. 1444-1510

132. The Dominican order

133. Michelangelo and Raphael

134. Dr. Fabrizio Mancinelli, curator of medieval and modern art at The Vatican Museums

135. May 8, 1508, to October 31, 1512

136. *Tradizioni*

137. Dante

138. Essentially, that a republican form of government should be governed under a system of natural law. In other words, to govern well, nations must respect the higher authority of God.

139. Cesare Porta

140. Vincenzo Bellini

141. Gaetano Donizetti

142. 1889 in Milan

143. Nineteenth-century Japan

144. Gian Carlo Menotti

145. In St. Petersburg (now Leningrad), Russia, 1862

146. 1865

147. "Pace, Mio Dio"

148. Victor Hugo

149. Felice Romani

150. Salvatore Cammanaro

151. Gioachino Rossini

152. Eighteenth-century Naples

153. La Scala

154. Between 1776 and 1778

155. Piermarini

156. La Fenice

157. In 1836 after the original one, built in 1790, burnt down. It was built by Giovanni Selva.

158. Teatro Dell'Opera—it was built by Achille Sfondrini in 1880.

159. After the Bourbon King Charles, who ordered its construction in 1737

160. La Scala was built on the site of an old church called Santa Maria della Scala, or Saint Mary of the Stairs.

161. The triumph of Caesar over Gaul

162. In May 1960, by Knights of Columbus Council 2105

163. Maria—among his famous works is *Cupid and Psyche.*

164. Verdi

165. George Washington—it is now displayed in the Gibbes Art Gallery in Charleston, South Carolina.

166. Guido Reni (1575-1642)

167. Black Belgium marble

168. Tennessee marble

169. Vincent Edwards, born Vincent Edward Zoino in 1928

170. In New Orleans in 1924

171. *Somebody Up There Likes Me*

172. Frankie Laine

173. "Mule Train," recorded in 1949

174. Elissa Landi

175. He completed a fresco there commemorating sixteenth-century Japanese Christian martyrs.

176. Mario Lanza

177. For the first time in history the director let the camera stay on close-up to an artist singing an aria. The artist was Mario Lanza, the aria, "Celeste Aida."

178. Rosa Zagnoni Marinoni

179. *Rebel Without a Cause*

180. March 12, 1946

181. Vincente Minnelli

182. Chicago

183. Michael A. Musmanno

184. Leonora in *La Forza del Destino*

185. John H. Secondari

186. His television productions and work as a foreign correspondent

187. Giorgio de Chirico

188. Claudio Monteverdi, who wrote *Orfeo* in 1607

189. Pietro Francesco Cavalli, with his opera *The Golden Apple.* It was writtten in honor of the marriage of Emperor Leopold I and performed in Vienna in 1667.

190. Italian keyboard composer

191. Venice

192. Yes—he made his debut in that field in 1981 in Seattle.

193. Ron Gaylord is Rinaldo Fredianelli, while Burt Holiday is Bonaldo Bonaldi.

194. *The Adventures of Pinocchio,* by Carlo Collodi. The translation is:

"There was once. . .a king!—quickly answer me my readers. No, you have made a mistake. There was once a piece of wood."

195. Sixteen

196. Weekly Italian newspapers published in the United States around the turn-of-the century

197. From 1926 to 1948

198. The Hoboken Four

199. A character portrayed in skits by the famous Italian-American comedian Farfariello. The character was always in some kind of trouble, hence the Neapolitan dialect word "Passaguai."

200. All wrote important books on the Vietnam War.

201. Father Benedict Sestini, in the nineteenth century

202. Montorio Nei Frentani, Italy

203. June 30, 1497

204. September 13, 1923

205. Maestro Gaetano Merola, who chose *La Boheme* for its first work

206. Ettore Ximenes

207. Pompeo Coppini

208. Gasparo Bertolotti from the town of Salo

209. At the straw market in Florence

210. Luigi Maggi, with his *Last Days of Pompeii* in 1908, and Enrico Guazzoni, with *Quo Vadis* in 1912

211. This Italian troupe is famous for their per-

formances of Renaissance plays.

212. Maria Vecchione of New Jersey

213. Sandro Botticelli (1444-1510)

214. Fra Filippo Lippi

215. Julius Caesar's *Commentaries on the Gallic War*

216. Federico Fellini

217. 1953 and 1954, respectively

218. Lotto (1970), Giorgione (1971), Ghirlandaio (1975), della Robbia (1978), Botticelli (1981) and della Robbia (1985)

219. Antonietta Pisanelli, in 1905

220. Edoardo Migliaccio

221. October 12, 1935, in Modena, Italy

222. Adele Venturi

223. Adua Veroni, in 1961

224. As Rodolfo in *La Boheme*

225. *Yes, Giorgio*

226. Knighthood and chivalry

227. Sofia Scicolone

228. D.H. Lawrence

229. The 1890s

230. Renata Scotto

231. *More Than a Diva*

232. The Italian national anthem "Italy" (Inno di Mameli), by Michele Novaro (1822-1885), adopted as the anthem June 2, 1946, on the establishment of the Italian Republic

No odyssey has been written so packed with incident as the annals of Italian cooking. If the entire fabric of this most varied of all cuisines could be laid out before our mind's eye, we would be faced with a tapestry of unequalled intricacy.

Marcella Hazan

Customs & Cuisine

1. What is the best-selling brand of olive oil in the United States?

2. Which Italian product must—by law—have less than 1-percent acidity?

3. Which grape is used to produce the Italian red wine Barbaresco?

4. Where is pasta made with apple and brandy a popular dish?

5. Where are the headquarters for the food firms of Motta and Alemagna?

6. What is a *taralli*?

7. If you were being served a plate of *zup-*

pa di patate, carciofi, e piselli, what would you be eating?

8. What is *risu niuru* or *riso nero?*

9. Who founded the Italian Swiss Colony Wine Company?

10. What was the original name of the Italian Swiss Colony Wine Company?

11. In what year was the famous Perugina chocolate and confections company established?

12. The feast of San Paolino is celebrated by Italians of what background?

13. Where is the feast of San Silverio celebrated?

14. Who was known as "the noodle priest"?

15. One of the biggest Italian feasts in the United States is the feast of San Gennaro in New York City. Can you name the church where the shrine of St. Gennaro is located?

16. What food item is fast replacing the hot dog as the symbol of American food, according to many culinary experts?

17. Who was the general manager of the famous New York restaurant Mamma Leone?

18. Who founded the first macaroni factory in Buffalo, New York?

19. What is Tuscany's number-one wine?

20. Name the company that is the largest manufacturer of spumoni and biscuit tortoni, among other ice cream products, in the nation.

21. When Italians ask for coffee, they usually want ______________ .

22. What city in Italy is noted for its delicious chocolates?

23. What is the name of the mythical person who brings gifts to Italian children?

24. In New Orleans, what is traditionally baked, especially by Sicilians, on St. Joseph's Day?

25. From what town in Italy did Pollio, the well-known cheese manufacturer, come?

26. What month is usually celebrated as American-Italian Culture and Heritage Month?

27. At what time of year is the *zampogna* played, especially in rural parts of Italy?

28. From where in Italy did the Ronzoni family—of macaroni fame—come?

29. Who is credited with introducing spumoni to America?

30. If someone served you *vermicelli alle vongolo*, what would you find mixed in with the pasta?

31. The noon-time meal of Italians is called ____________________ .

32. *Pizza di grano* is a favorite food served at what time of year?

33. Which American restaurant was the very first to issue a printed menu?

34. When an Italian sends you good wishes, he says, __________________ .

35. What is the usual greeting when an Italian picks up the phone?

36. What are *struffoli?*

37. Who started the Christmas custom of putting up a creche to commemorate the birth of the Christ Child?

38. What is considered the most important red wine produced in Verona?

39. What is Granduca Cortese Di Gavi?

40. A *pizzelle* most closely resembles what American food item?

41. For what is the town of Gorgonzola near Milan famous?

42. Where and when is the Polenta Fair in Italy?

43. What is *polenta?*

44. What are *gnocchi di patate?*

45. What are *melanzane ripieni?*

46. What is the family name of the man who opened the first Italian restaurant in Egypt in the very early 1900s?

47. Alfredo is the name of a well-known restaurant in Rome and the United States. What is the last name of the individual who opened his famous restaurant in Rome in 1914?

48. Name the two actors who first gave him the title "Alfredo, the King of Pasta."

49. If you should see a restaurant advertising itself as *Vera Cucina Italiana,* what does its owner claim?

50. When do you hear the greeting "*Buon Natale*"?

51. When do you hear the greeting "*Felice Capo d'Anno*"?

52. Where in Italy is the Festival of the Two Worlds held?

53. What western Sicilian city bears the same name as a sweet wine?

54. What is usually celebrated in Siena on July 2 and August 16?

55. If the words *al forno* are found after a menu item, how was the dish cooked?

56. Many Italians like to put some anisette or sambuca liqueur into ____________ .

57. If *pane* is Italian for "bread," what does the phrase *pane di casa signify?*

58. What is *insalata di mare*?

59. Different types of pizzas have been around for centuries. However, in the eighteenth century, Neapolitans introduced what ingredient without which we wouldn't recognize pizza today?

60. What is signified when someone says a type of cooking is *casalinga?*

61. After whom is the "Margherita" pizza named?

62. What is a *pizzaiolo?*

63. Does the United States or Italy produce more mozzarella?

64. Who is credited with first putting mozzarella on pizza?

65. Who is credited with opening the first pizzeria in the United States?

66. Why was the *calzone,* which means "pants leg," so named?

67. Even though cake or other sweets may be available, what is the most preferred finale to an Italian meal in Italy?

68. What is a *minestre*?

69. What is *sorbetto al melone*?

70. *Linguine* is a form of pasta. How does the word translate?

71. How do Italians spell the word macaroni?

72. Elena is another form of pasta. After whom was it named?

73. How does *cappelli di prete* translate?

74. Who in the United States received the first permit to dispense fish cocktails for his San Francisco restaurant?

75. What is a *frittata*?

76. What is the name of the popular Italian green used for salad?

77. Match the following names and types of pasta to the appropriate picture:

1) Anellini
2) Farfalle
3) Cavatelli
4) Creste di Galli
5) Ditali
6) Fettuccine
7) Funghini
8) Fusilli
9) Maruzze rigati
10) Lasagne riccie
11) Lumachine
12) Mafalde
13) Rigatoni
14) Rotelle
15) Semi di melone
16) Occhi di lupo
17) Orzo
18) Ravioli
19) Stellini
20) Tubetti
21) Ziti Rigati
22) Vermicelli
23) Tortellini

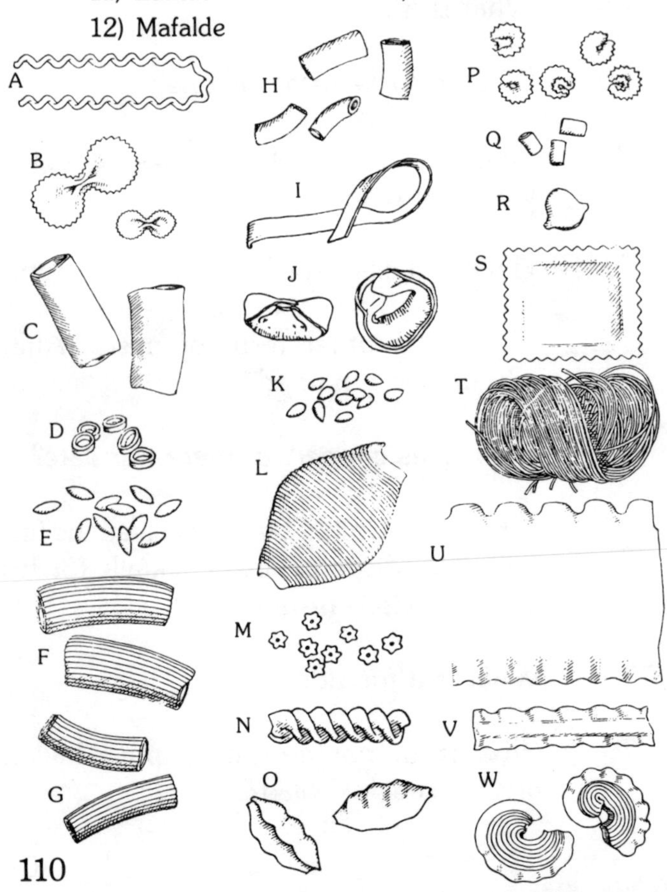

Answers

1. Bertolli, from the area of Lucca in the province of Tuscany

2. Extra virgin olive oil

3. Nebbiolo

4. Vincenza

5. Milan

6. It is a kind of biscuit, especially popular in Naples.

7. A soup consisting of potatoes, artichokes, and peas—basically a Neopolitan dish

8. "Black rice" is a Sicilian Christmas dessert,

especially in the area around Messina, Sicily. The first spelling is dialect, the second, Italian. Essentially, it is rice in a mixture of chocolate, citron and almonds.

9. Andrea Sbarboro

10. The Italian Swiss Agricultural Association, incorporated on March 10, 1881

11. In 1907 in Perugia, Italy

12. Those from Nola

13. The island of Ponza

14. Msgr. John Romaniello (1917-1985), a Maryknoll priest who established noodle factories in Hong Kong to help the poor

15. The Church of the Most Precious Blood

16. Pizza

17. Bruno Bernabo

18. Pietro Catalano, just before the turn of the century

19. Chianti

20. Sedutto

21. An espresso

22. Perugia

23. La Befana

24. St. Joseph's bread, in various shapes and sizes

25. Giuseppe Pollio hailed from Sorrento.

26. October

27. The *zampogna,* or Italian bagpipe, is played by shepherds especially at Christmas in honor of the Christ Child.

28. San Fruttuoso, near Genoa

29. Frank Cotillo of East Harlem in New York City, back in the 1890s. Before emigrating to this country, he had owned large confectionery shops in the Galleria Umberto I in Naples.

30. Clams

31. *colazione*

32. "Grain pie" is traditionally served at Easter.

33. Delmonico's Restaurant at 494 Pearl Street in New York City in 1834—a cup of coffee or a cup of tea could be had for one cent. A bowl of either drink, if you wanted to splurge, would cost two cents.

34. *"Auguri"*

35. *"Pronto"*

36. Delicious little balls of dough covered with

honey and sprinkles and baked especially for holidays

37. St. Francis of Assisi

38. Valpolicella

39. A white wine produced in the Piedmont region of Italy

40. A waffle

41. Sharp blue cheese

42. The Polenta Fair is held in the town of Casorzo in the province of Asti in November.

43. Cornmeal mush

44. Potato dumplings

45. Stuffed eggplant

46. Migliucci

47. De Lelio

48. Mary Pickford and Douglas Fairbanks, in 1927

49. That only authentic Italian cooking is done there

50. Christmas

51. New Year's Day

52. Spoleto

53. Marsala

54. *Corsa del Palio,* or "Parade of the Banner"

55. "In the oven"

56. espresso

57. The bread is "homemade."

58. Seafood salad

59. The tomato

60. It's home-style cooking.

61. The late-nineteenth-century queen of Italy

62. A cook who specializes in pizza

63. The United States

64. Raffaele Esposito, a Neopolitan

65. Gennaro Lombardi in New York City's "Little Italy" in 1905, ten years after he had arrived from Naples

66. Because it resembled a leg of the baggy

trousers worn by Neapolitan men in the late eighteenth and early nineteenth centuries

67. Fruit

68. A soup

69. Cantaloupe sherbet

70. "Small tongues"

71. *Maccheroni*

72. Queen Elena of Italy

73. "Priests' hats," another form of pasta

74. Tomaso Castagnola, in 1916

75. An omelet

76. Cicoria (dandelion)

77. Answers:

1) D
2) B
3) O
4) W
5) H
6) I
7) P
8) A
9) L
10) U
11) R
12) V
13) F
14) N
15) K
16) C
17) E
18) S
19) M
20) Q
21) G
22) T
23) J

Once I thought to write a history of the immigrants in America. Then I discovered that the immigrants were American history.

Oscar Handlin

Arrivederci Italia—Immigration

1. What Italian missionary and explorer of the western United States is honored in Washington D.C.'s National Statuary Hall?

2. Name the two Italian-born priests who founded St. Ignatius College in California in the mid-nineteenth century.

3. ________________ was an Italian-born missionary nun—a Sister of Mercy—who spent some twenty years on the frontiers of Colorado and New Mexico, meeting Billy the Kid on her travels.

4. Who founded the city of Buffalo, New York?

5. When was the Italian book publishing firm of S.F. Vanni, New York City, established?

6. Name the Italian priest who in the 1890s brought about thirty-five Italian families to Arkansas and founded the town of Tontitown.

7. The Carson family founded a community in California in 1905. After what Italian city did they name it?

8. Who was the first white child born in Detroit, Michigan?

9. What is the town of Loretto, Pennsylvania, named after?

10. Name the city in Pennsylvania whose inhabitants are almost 100-percent Italian.

11. What is the historical significance of St. Mary Magdalene de Pazzi Church?

12. Who was the first pastor of St. Mary Magdalene de Pazzi?

13. What is the anti-defamation arm of the Order of the Sons of Italy called?

14. What town in Missouri is named after an eighteenth-century Italian saint who founded a religious order?

15. What is the Italian-American community of Boston called?

16. What is the Italian community of Chicago called?

17. When was the Order of the Sons of Italy established?

18. What is the Italian section of Pittsburgh called?

19. Name the son of an Italian immigrant who was the highest-ranking naval officer of Italian descent to serve in the U.S. Navy in the Civil War.

20. It is estimated that about 9.5 million immigrants arrived in the United States between 1880 and 1900. How many came from Italy?

21. Why should there be a county in Indiana called Vigo?

22. "In fond memory of my beloved and unforgettable parents who taught me the religion of God and the religion of work. I dedicate this . . . enterprise in the New World." Who is the author of this quote? Where is it displayed?

23. Who was the first naturalized American to be canonized a saint?

24. Where was the first monument to Christopher Columbus erected?

25. Which was the first Italian-language newspaper published in the United States?

26. What is the Italian-American section of Providence, Rhode Island, called?

27. Approximately how many Italians emigrated from Italy to the United States between 1820 to 1850?

28. In what year did Giuseppe Garibaldi arrive in New York?

29. Who designed the Statue of Liberty?

30. After whom is Ravalli County in Montana named?

31. When did Italian Franciscan priests first settle in New York State?

32. Name the Italian who signed the Declaration of Independence.

33. Who is the dean of Italian-American historians?

34. To what area do most of the Italian-Americans in Louisiana trace their ancestry?

35. The pioneer Catholic missionary in the west and southwest was __________.

36. The pioneer missionary in the midwest was ______________________________.

37. Who founded St. Bonaventure College in Upstate New York?

38. In 1930, what two states bordering New York had the greatest number of naturalized citizens of Italian background?

39. A great Italian language newspaper for immigrants in the United States is *Il Progresso Italo-Americano.* Another famous newspaper, similar in scope and issued by the same publisher, is now no longer in print. Name paper and publisher.

40. Who created the cartoon characters of Tom and Jerry, The Flintstones, and Papa Smurf?

41. In 1900 the government kept records to show the amount of money that immigrants were bringing into the country. Was the per capita amount brought by those from southern Italy above or below $100?

42. The phrase *"Pane e lavoro"* symbolized ____________________.

43. What was the peak year of Italian emigration to the United States?

44. In 1985 were there any native Japanese missionaries working in Italy, and if so, how many?

45. What two Latin American countries attracted the most Italian emigrants?

46. What name did Argentinians give to Italian migrant workers who came to their country in the latter half of the nineteenth-century to harvest wheat?

47. Were most immigrants to Argentina from the north or south of Italy?

48. Which Brazilian city has the highest concentration of Italians?

49. What was the occupation of most Italians in Brazil before World War I?

50. What was a man called who served as a labor broker to recruit immigrants laborers for the United States?

51. He was a Dutch-born journalist in early twentieth-century New York who did much to bring the plight of poor immigrants of all nationalities to the public's attention. Who was he?

52. According to the 1980 census, where do those of Italian background rank in size in the total population (from one to ten)?

53. For what is the firm Capezio known?

54. What does CIAA stand for?

55. Who was the first Italian missionary to be martyred in this country?

56. Approximately how many different American Indian languages did Father Joseph Cataldo, an early pioneer Catholic missionary, master?

57. "*Trenta giorni di nave a vapore*" were words in a song sung by whom?

58. The Saint Raphael Italian Benevolent Society was established in 1891 to aid immigrants who had just arrived from Italy. Who founded it?

59. Who was the first Catholic missionary to die in lower California?

60. Name the missionary credited with discovering what is today Arizona.

61. In what city was Father Angelo Paresce, founder of Woodstock College in Maryland, born?

62. Who was the Commissioner General of Immigration from 1913 to 1921?

63. When did the Italian Lazarists fathers first come to the United States?

64. Who founded the first Catholic church in what is now the Bronx in New York?

65. When did the Missionary Sisters of the Order of Saint Charles leave Italy to work in Brazil?

66. Who was the first Italian-American bishop in the Archdiocese of New York?

67. What Italian was the bishop of Savannah? Where was he born?

68. In what year was the Casa Italiana, at Columbia University, established?

69. What was the name of the first Italian ethnic parish in Chicago?

70. Of all the Italians who were the first settlers in Milwaukee, approximately what percentage were from Sicily?

71. Name the two oldest ethnic national churches attended by New York City Italians.

72. Many books have been published dealing with the Italian-American's experience as an immigrant. Match the following five titles with their authors.

1) *The Italian Immigrant Woman in North America* (1978)
2) *The Franciscans and Italian Immigration in America* (1977)
3) *The Immigrants Speak, Italian Americans Tell Their Story* (1979)

a. Betty Boyd Caroli, Robert F. Harney and Lydio F. Tomasi
b. Lydio F. Tomasi
c. Andrew F. Rolle
d. Leonard F. Bacigalupo
e. Salvatore J. LaGumina

4) *The Immigrant Upraised—Italian Adventures and Colonists in an expanding America* (1968)
5) *Italian Americans—New Perspectives in Italian Immigration and Ethnicity* (1985)

73. Name the former mayor of Franklin, Pennsylvania, who had the longest tenure of any mayor in that state.

74. Who was Orson Welles' card and magic teacher?

75. What is the title of the book published in 1961 by Gay Talese describing the history of *The New York Times?*

76. What was Frank Sinatra's first hit record?

77. Whom did Frank Sinatra marry in 1939?

78. Where was football commissioner Pete Rozelle born?

79. Who played the role of Pookie Adams in the movie *The Sterile Cuckoo?*

80. Who wrote *A Passion for Sicilians* and *America Is Also Italian?*

81. Who was the Italian-born actress who starred in Cecil B. DeMille's 1932 epic, *The Sign of the Cross?*

82. In what city in Vermont did many Italian stonecutters settle?

83. Who named the town of Lodi, Texas?

84. Where in the U.S. is a small town named after a pope?

85. After whom was Beltrami County in Minnesota named?

86. Name the first woman of Italian background to receive an M.D. degree from the Women's Medical College in Philadelphia.

87. A signer of the Declaration of Independence was married to a woman with some Italian blood. Who was the signer, and what his wife's name?

88. In 1966, 7.8 percent of all immigrants to the United States were Italian. To what percentage did it shrink ten years later in 1976?

89. Name the five states in which most Italian immigrants settled between 1966 and 1976.

90. How many of the chief executive officers and board members of this country's eight

hundred largest corporations are Italian-Americans?

91. According to the 1924 National Origins Act, which set up restrictive quotas for all immigrants to this country, how many Italians could emigrate?

92. In terms of income, name the five richest cities in Italy.

93. What is the address of the famous Ferrara's Pastry Shop in New York City?

94. Who was the first Italian-American appointed to the New Jersey Supreme Court?

95. What Italian-American starred in the popular T.V. series "Welcome Back Kotter"?

96. What disease rampant in southern Italy in the latter part of the nineteenth century induced many Italians to emigrate?

97. What percentage of the quarter of a million members of the International Ladies Garment Workers Union of Greater New York were of Italian background in the 1930s?

98. In New York City during the first half of the twentieth century, most of the icemen were Italians from what province?

99. Who is credited with being the first lawyer of Italian background in New York City?

100. What year did Washington Irving visit Italy?

101. In what Italian city did the nineteenth-century writer William Dean Howells serve as American consul?

102. Name the first Italian-produced movie to be exhibited in New York City.

103. Name the Italian at the 1932 Los Angeles Olympics.

104. Name the dental scientist who in 1983 was honored by Columbia University for his research over the years culminating in the cataloging of over four hundred separate disease entities.

105. Was the New York City annual Columbus Day Parade ever canceled?

106. What was the main job of Italian migrants to Nevada in the 1880s?

107. Who founded the lawn-care franchise The Lawn Doctor?

108. At what university was Alpha Phi Delta, an Italian-American fraternity, started?

109. Name the Italian scholar who in the 1920s explored Nepal and Tibet and translated works from Sanskrit and Tibetan.

110. Who was the founder of the Yoo-Hoo Beverage Company?

111. For how many years did Alfredo Antonini conduct the CBS Symphony for radio and television?

112. After World War II, to what two European countries did many Italians emigrate?

113. How did the term "taxi" originate?

114. What is the first name of New York governor Mario Cuomo's wife?

115. Only one family in the United States ever had five of its sons in the priesthood. Who were they?

116. What Italian star made the song "Volare" so popular?

117. Name the first Italian-American to become chief of detectives in the New York City Police Department.

Answers

1. The Jesuit priest Eusebio Chino (His name often appears as King.)

2. Father Michael Accolti and Father Anthony Marasci—the college later became the University of San Francisco.

3. Sister Blandina Segale (1850-1941)

4. Paolo Busti, who was born in Milan in the mid-1700s

5. 1884

6. Father Pietro Bandini

7. Naples

8. Teresa Tonti

9. The shrine of the same name in Italy

10. Roseto, named after a town in the province of Foggia

11. It was the first Italian ethnic parish in this country, established in Philadelphia in 1852.

12. Father Gaetano Mariani

13. National Commission of Social Justice

14. The town of Liguori, which was named after St. Alphonsus Liguori (1696-1787), founder of the Redemptorist Order, founder of modern moral theology, and author of over one hundred books.

15. The North End

16. The Near West Side

17. 1905

18. Bloomfield

19. Rear Admiral Bancroft Gherardi, who in 1887 became commander-in-chief of the North Atlantic Squadron

20. About 1 million

21. To honor Colonel Francis Vigo, who in the eighteenth century aided Rogers and

Clark in their exploration of the Northwest Territory

22. Giovanni Buitoni, who within a decade of coming to America opened his pasta business. The plaque is in the Buitoni pasta factory in New Jersey.

23. Mother Frances Xavier Cabrini, founder of the Institute of the Missionary Sisters of the Sacred Heart, canonized by Pope Pius XII on July 7, 1946

24. In Baltimore, dedicated on October 12, 1792, to honor the 300th anniversary of the discovery of America

25. *L'Eco d'Italia,* published in 1849

26. Federal Hill

27. 4,561

28. 1849

29. Federic Bartholdi, whose family emigrated from Italy to France

30. Father Anthony Ravalli (1827-1884), a missionary who built the first flour mill in Montana

31. 1855

32. William Paca

33. The late Giovanni Schiavo

34. Sicily

35. Father Eusebio Chino

36. Father Samuel Mazzuchelli

37. Franciscan Father Pamphilus de Magliano

38. Pennsylvania followed by New Jersey

39. *Il Corriere d'America,* published by Generoso Pope

40. Joe Barbera, of Hanna-Barbera Productions

41. Far below. To be specific, Southern Italians brought in only $8.84 per capita, third lowest from the bottom. The Scots came in with the highest amount—$41.51 per capita.

42. The spirit of emigration: to find work and make a living. It translates "Bread and work."

43. 1907

44. Yes—there were ten, this as a gesture of gratitude from the Catholics of Japan for bringing the Catholic faith from the West to the East. There were, incidentally, fifteen Japanese priests working in the U.S.

45. Argentina and Brazil

46. *Golondrinas* or "swallows"

47. The north

48. Sao Paulo

49. Most were laborers on coffee plantations.

50. A *padrone*

51. Jacob A. Riis

52. They are the sixth largest ancestry group, or about one in every twenty individuals in the country.

53. Capezio is the foremost manufacturer of ballet shoes. It was founded in 1887 by Salvatore Capezio after he emigrated from Murolucano.

54. The Coalition of Italo-American Associations

55. Father Linares, in 1571

56. Twenty

57. "Thirty days of steamship travel" were words from a song sung by Italian emigrants during the end of the nineteenth century and the early twentieth-century.

58. Father Pietro Bandini, a Scalabrini priest

59. Father Francisco Piccolo, who came from Palermo in 1654

60. Father Marco da Nizza

61. Naples

62. Anthony Caminetti

63. They landed in Baltimore in 1816.

64. Father Felix Villanis, a native of Italy, in 1845. In 1841 he helped found what was to become Fordham University.

65. 1895

66. The late Bishop Joseph Pernicone

67. Bishop Ignazio Persico (1823-1896), who was born in Naples

68. 1914

69. Our Lady of the Assumption, established in 1886

70. 65 percent

71. Old Saint Patrick's Cathedral and Saint Anthony's Shrine Church

72. 1. a
    2. d
    3. e
    4. c
    5. b

73. Mayor Guy Mammolite

74. John Scarne

75. *The Kingdom and the Power*

76. "I'll Never Smile Again"

77. Nancy Barbato

78. South Gate, California, on March 1, 1926

79. Liza Minnelli

80. Jerre Mangione

81. Elissa Landi

82. Barre

83. J. Lopresto, who wanted to perpetuate the name of his birthplace in Italy

84. In Macon County, Georgia, the village of Pio Nono is named for Pope Pius IX.

85. Constantino Beltrami (1779-1885), an early explorer of the area

86. Annina Carmela Rondinella, who received it in 1899

87. George Wythe of Virginia was married to Elizabeth Taliaferro, whose family had come to the area in the 1650s.

88. 2.1 percent

89. In order, they were New York, New Jersey, Illinois, Massachusetts and Connecticut.

90. Only 3.2 percent

91. Only 3,845 per year

92. In order, they are Milan, Bologna, Florence, Turin and Bari.

93. 195-201 Grand Street

94. Marie Garibaldi

95. John Travolta

96. Malaria

97. About 40 percent

98. Apulia—no one knows why because Apulians did not even have ice.

99. Carlo Antonio Rapallo, who was born in the city in 1832

100. 1804

101. Venice, in 1861

102. *Queen of the Roses* (1916)

103. Luigi Beccali

104. Dr. Edward Zegarelli, who taught for forty-one years at Columbia

105. Yes, in 1983 out of respect for Terrence Cardinal Cooke, whose death had occurred a few days earlier

106. To man huge kilns used to produce charcoal for smelters

107. Anthony Giordano, in 1965

108. Syracuse University, in 1914

109. Guiseppe Tucci

110. Albert V. Olivieri

111. Thirty years

112. France and Swizterland, in that order

113. It derived from the family of the sixteenth-century Italian poet Torquato Tasso, which emigrated to Germany, changed its name to the Germanic form "Taxis," and started the business of transporting things from one area to another.

114. Matilda

115. The Farina family, who gave sons Edward, Joseph, Wilfred, Albert and Louis—all diocesan priests

116. Domenico Modugno

117. Richard Nicastro, appointed in 1984

The Italians who reached the New World, starting with Columbus, were usually outsiders struggling against great odds, and the best of them were brave, beautiful human beings full of warmth and a large-hearted concern for humanity.

Eril Amfitheatrof

Italians in America

1. Who organized the "Wear a Rose for Life" campaign to combat pro-abortionists?

2. Name the Italian-American who served as Secretary of the Navy.

3. Who was the United States Attorney General in the years 1978 to 1981?

4. Who visited President Franklin Pierce in 1853 and touched off a wave of violent anti-Catholic demonstrations?

5. Who was the literary editor of the famous Boston newspaper *The Pilot* in the mid-nineteenth century?

6. What was the maiden name of the first woman to be elected governor of a state in her own right?

7. Name the chief organist at St. Patrick's Cathedral in New York City between 1927 and 1943.

8. Who established the Garibaldi-Meucci Museum in New York City?

9. Who was the founder of the Department of Mechanical Engineering at the prestigious Massachusetts Institute of Technology?

10. Name the individual who, after a long and tedious battle, helped convince officials in Colorado to have Columbus Day proclaimed a legal holiday?

11. Who was the first Catholic priest to be appointed Chaplain of the United States Senate?

12. Whom does the Robert S. Maestri Bridge in Louisiana honor?

13. Who is honored by the city of Rosati, Missouri?

14. Who founded the United Fruit Company?

15. Name the popular basketball coach at St. John's University in Jamaica, New York,

who led his teams to so many victories?

16. What is the nickname of former world lightweight boxing champion Ray Mancini?

17. Who was the founding editor of the journal *Italian Americana?*

18. What modern Italian-American is considered to be the greatest American translator of Italian poetry?

19. When was the Italian Teachers Association formed?

20. In 1920, which was the only public high school in the country to teach Italian?

21. Who was the famous sixteenth-century architect who influenced American colonial architecture?

22. According to the 1980 census, which state has the highest percentage of Italian background and which the lowest?

23. Who was inaugurated as president of Yale University in 1978?

24. In what year was the famous Perillo Tours Company formed?

25. A unique repository of archival materials, as well as published reports, monographs

and books dealing with Italian-Americans is found in what part of New York City?

26. In 1980 a hospital in New York City created the only hospital-based hospice with an in-patient unit dedicated exclusively to the care of the terminally ill. Name the hospital.

27. Name the poet and labor leader who was involved in the famous 1912 textile strike in Lawrence, Massachusetts.

28. Who created the character E.T.?

29. Who was the first Italian-American to be elected to Congress?

30. Who built the first large vessel ever to sail on the Great Lakes?

31. "All men are by nature equally free and independent. This quality is essential to the establishment of a liberal government." Did Thomas Jefferson make this statement?

32. Who was the first director of the famous Metropolitan Museum of Art of New York City, and for what was he famous?

33. Of whom was the Italian ambassador to the United States speaking when he said, "I consider the illustrious Mother General

of the Missionary Sisters of the Sacred Heart a priceless collaborator, for while I work for the interest of Italy among the powerful, she succeeds in making it loved and esteemed by the humble, the infirm, and the children"?

34. "The Bank for Just Plain Folks"—is this a modern-day slogan?

35. When did Marconi receive his patent on his invention of the wireless?

36. What was an earlier name for Radio Corporation of America (RCA), and in what state was it incorporated?

37. What is actor Don Ameche's middle name?

38. Who was the original Jack Armstrong on radio?

39. How many winners did Eddie Arcaro, the famous jockey, ride during his career?

40. Eddie Arcaro won two Triple Crowns. Name the years and the horses he rode.

41. What was the real name of the great bodybuilder Charles Atlas?

42. Where and when was singer Frankie Avalon born?

43. What is Yogi Berra's real name, and where was he born?

44. Who is the most decorated policeman in New York State?

45. Where and when was the actor Ernest Borgnine born?

46. How many times was Frank Capra president of the Academy of Motion Pictures?

47. Name the first Italian-American to be appointed Secretary of Health, Education and Welfare.

48. Which American college was the first to offer instruction in the Italian language, and who taught the course?

49. Name the pope who created the first Catholic diocese in the United States.

50. On April 22, 1964, the New York City World's Fair was dedicated and opened. Who performed the introductory music at this event?

51. What is the Italian section of St. Louis called?

52. Where was the Genovese Pharmacy chain opened?

53. Which twentieth-century president went to an Italian barber during the last seven years of his life, and what was his name?

54. What was the former name of 164th Street in Jamaica, New York?

55. In what year was famous shortstop Phil Rizzuto elected Most Valuable Player in the American League?

56. What popular "Irish" politician—and the first Catholic to run for president—was Italian on his father's side? Where was his father born?

57. What was the name of the Civil War Union Army unit composed mainly of Italian-American volunteers?

58. What is the address of the Italian embassy in Washington, D.C.?

59. Who is the national historian of the Sons of Italy?

60. For what National League team did Joe DiMaggio's brother play?

61. What is the family name of the well-known, nation-wide moving company started by seven brothers?

62. Name the Italian-named top-ranking firework company in the U.S.

63. Who was the founder of the first large-scale broccoli farm in the United States?

64. Who said, "It's ability, not disability, that counts"?

65. Who was the late wife of columnist Jimmy Breslin?

66. Who said, "A better world begins with me"?

67. What college did Geraldine Ferraro attend?

68. Who, in 1957, founded the Key Food Stores supermarket chain?

69. What Italian-American received a patent for the telephone in 1871?

70. Name the first Italian-American to be elected Mayor of Philadelphia.

71. Name the first Italian-American to be appointed to the New York City Police force.

72. A star of the television series "Taxi," he now has a successful movie career. He is married to Rhea Pearlman of "Cheers" fame. Who is he?

73. Who holds the New York Rangers goaltending record for most shutouts, wins and assists?

74. When did Yankee catcher Yogi Berra re-

ceive the American League Most Valuable Player Award?

75. Where was maestro Arturo Toscanini born?

76. When was comedian Lou Costello born?

77. Who painted *The Apotheosis of Washington*, the fresco on the capitol dome?

78. Name the year and the street on which the great Jimmy Durante was born.

79. Name the aide to George Rogers Clark who explored the Northwest Territory in the late eighteenth century.

80. When was the Italian Welfare League founded?

81. What sport did the late Guy Lombardo love?

82. Who was the young, popular singer of the 1970s who sometimes performed under the stage name Johnny Baron?

83. Since 1972, what Italian-American has been in charge of keeping the torch of the Statue of Liberty free from dirt and dust?

84. Who was the top horse-racing handicapper for the old *New York Mirror* and the *New York News?*

85. When was the first time that an American stamp was issued based on a child's art work, and what did it commemorate?

86. Who was the trainer for such boxing champions as Floyd Patterson, Gene Tunney, and Jersey Joe Walcott?

87. What was the late Fiorello LaGuardia's sister's name?

88. Name the first aviator to transmit a message via radio from his aircraft to a ground station.

89. Was Dennis Demisposa ever a popular television host?

90. Peter Sammartino founded what New Jersey university?

91. In 1935 a judge did not permit the public to attend a civil separation case between a noted crooner and his estranged wife in order not to turn the atmosphere into one of a circus. Name the crooner and the judge.

92. Who was the co-sponsor of a 1955 New York State bill to establish middle-income housing projects?

93. In 1984 a commencement address was

delivered in, of all languages, Latin. Name the university and the orator.

94. In 1914, the state militia in a western state killed eleven Italian men, women and children in an effort to break a strike. Name the state and the occupation in which the Italian men were engaged.

95. What percentage of the U.S. forces fighting in World War I were Italian-Americans? How many received the DSC?

96. Five Sicilian shopkeepers were lynched by a mob in Tallulah, Louisiana, at the turn of the century. Why?

97. What modern biochemist developed the drugs Acerbine and Cerbartrol?

98. In what section of New York City was Bernadette Peters born?

99. When was the National Italian-American Sports Hall of Fame established?

100. Name the five individuals honored in 1985 by the NIASHF.

101. U.S. Patent No. 53,165 was issued to Antonio Meucci on December 28, 1871, for his invention of ______________ .

102. This Italian-born Salesian priest now

working in the United States is a recognized expert on the Shroud of Turin. Name him.

103. Name the priest who in the 1960s led the civil rights battle in Milwaukee and who was named by the Associated Press as the religious newsmaker of 1967.

104. What is the name of the American organization which helps maintain the Casa Guidi in Florence?

105. Who is the president of "Columbus Countdown 1992"?

106. Who was the first recipient of the "Columbus Countdown 1992" award?

107. What is the purpose of "Columbus Countdown 1992"?

108. Where is the headquarters of the American Labor Museum?

109. Who was the great bishop of Milan who in the fourth century converted Augustine, later to become St. Augustine?

110. Why should Tampa have a street named Adamo Drive?

111. After which Roman church was the Cathedral of Saints Peter and Paul in Philadelphia designed?

112. Who was the founder of the Society of the Catholic Apostolate, better known as the Pallottine Fathers?

113. Who was elected governor of Massachusetts in 1956?

114. Name the popular magazine for Italian-Americans published in New York.

115. Only one mayor in New York City's history succeeded in defeating the nominees of both the Democratic and Republican parties. He ran on the Experience Party ticket in 1949. Name him.

116. Who were the two candidates of the major parties—both Italian-Americans—he defeated?

117. What was Rocky Marciano's major achievement in boxing?

118. Where was Marciano born?

119. Who were his manager and trainer when he began his career?

120. Marciano said, "It was the saddest punch of my life. How else could I feel seeing . . . one of the finest sportsmen that ever lived lying there on the canvas?" On what occasion?

121. This architect and urban planner built an

"earth house" in Scottsdale, Arizona, constructed from desert materials and advanced new concepts in architecture. Name him.

122. Name the woman who was mayor of Hartford, Connecticut, in the late 1960s.

123. In what state was Frank Sinatra born?

124. What was the answer given by President Woodrow Wilson after hearing complaints that Italians were taking money out of the country by returning to their homeland after working here for a while?

125. In the tragedy of the great mine explosion in Cherry, Illinois, in 1909, about how many Italian workmen were killed?

126. "I have suffered because I was an Italian." Who said this?

127. What did Governor Michael Dukakis of Massachusetts proclaim on August 23, 1977, to avenge the memory of Sacco and Vanzetti?

128. Who was Willie La Morte?

129. Who was the first enlisted Marine to receive the Congressional Medal in World War II?

130. Who was the chairman of the House

Judiciary Committee during the historic Watergate case?

131. Who was the judge at the Watergate trial?

132. Which state did Senator Peter Domenici represent?

133. From which state did Congressman Frank Annunzio come?

134. Which president declared Columbus Day a national holiday?

135. Who was John Cappeletti?

136. On what team did Giorgio Chinaglia once play?

137. Who was the director of the Apollo Space Program?

138. "No man need restrict his desire to serve his fellow man to the number of formal hours he is required to put in at his job. The many ways in which we may render service for humanity are to be governed more by the laws of morality than by wage and hour laws. . . ." Who said this?

139. What Italian is honored on a United States airmail stamp?

140. Who was the recipient of the first National Italian-American Foundation Communications Scholarship Award?

141. Who is the publisher of the oldest Italian cultural magazine in the U.S., *La Follia*?

142. When was civil rights activist Viola Liuzzo of Detroit killed?

143. Who entered Boston Harbor in 1831 with fifty-three barrels of river salmon caught in the Columbia River in Washington State?

144. In what country was Guy Lombardo born?

145. The EPCOT Center in Florida features an Italian city as one of its foreign-country exhibits. Name the city.

146. Name the pioneer Texas aviator who later moved to Long Island, New York, and designed the UB-14B used during World War II?

147. Who is the publisher of *The New Yorker* magazine?

148. The Paulist Press, one of the largest religious book publishers, was known by another name from 1891 to 1913. What was it?

149. Name the football great who set championship game records in the early 1940s when he was with the Chicago Bears.

150. Name the state where in the 1890s Alessandro Mastro-Valerio founded two small agricultural colonies for Italian farmers.

151. Who is the editor of the magazine *Italy, Italy?*

152. Who was the international president of the St. Vincent de Paul Society in 1982 when it celebrated its 150th anniversary?

153. What is the name of the newspaper published for the Italian-American community in Milwaukee, Wisconsin?

154. In 1985, who was elected president of UNICO?

155. When was Al Pacino born?

156. What is the name of the Baltimore-born director of the Vatican Observatory?

157. Who was the first man of Italian background elected to the Senate?

158. Where was actor Frank Langella born?

159. Enrico Caruso's favorite hobby was caricature. Whom did he caricature in this picture?

Answers

1. Father Charles Fiore

2. Charles Bonaparte (1905-1906)

3. Benjamin Civiletti

4. Cardinal Gaetano Bedini, an emissary of Pope Pius IX

5. Father Joseph Mary Finotti (1817-1879), who also authored numerous Catholic biographies

6. Tambussi was the maiden name of Ella Grasso (1919-1981), governor of Connecticut.

7. Pietro Alessandro Yon (1886-1943). He wrote more than seventy church compositions, and in 1926 was named honorary music director of St. Peter's in Rome.

8. The Order of the Sons of Italy

9. Gaetano Lanza

10. Angelo Noce, who came from Genoa, the city of Columbus's birth

11. Father Charles Constantine Pise, in 1832

12. A former mayor of New Orleans

13. Bishop Joseph Rosati (1789-1834), who was the first Bishop of St. Louis

14. Joseph Di Giorgio

15. Lou Carnesecca

16. "Boom Boom"

17. The late Dr. Ernest Salvatore Falbo of Buffalo, New York

18. Dr. Joseph Tusiani, who was born in Italy but now resides in the Bronx

19. 1912

20. De Witt Clinton High School in the Bronx

21. Andrea Palladio of Vicenza, Italy (1518-1580)

22. Rhode Island with 19.5 percent has the highest, while the Dakotas, both North and South, share the lowest with only 0.6 percent.

23. Angelo Bartlett Giamatti

24. On May 30, 1945, in the Bronx, New York, by Joseph Perillo, father of Mario Perillo

25. The Center for Migration Studies is located on Staten Island.

26. The Cabrini Medical Center

27. Arturo Giovannitti

28. Carlo Rambaldi

29. Francis Spinola in 1887, who represented part of the Long Island area of New York State

30. Enrico Tonti, as an agent for France in 1679

31. No—Filippo Mazzei is the author. Jefferson incorporated the phrase, slightly altered, into the Declaration of Independence

32. Luigi Palma Di Cesnola. He was a noted archaeologist and uncovered much of

historical significance in the mid-nineteenth century on the Island of Cyprus.

33. Mother Frances Xavier Cabrini

34. No—it goes back at least to 1913 and was coined by Amadeo Peter Giannini in California for his Bank of Italy.

35. July 2, 1897

36. The Marconi Wireless Company of America, incorporated in New Jersey

37. Felix

38. Jim Ameche

39. 4,779

40. 1941 riding Whirlaway, 1948 riding Citation

41. Angelo Siciliano

42. In Philadelphia on September 8, 1940

43. Lawrence Peter Berra was born in St. Louis.

44. Congressman Mario Biaggi

45. Ermes Effron Borgnino was born in Hamden, Connecticut, in 1915.

46. Four

47. Anthony Celebrezze, who was appointed by President Kennedy in 1962

48. The College of William & Mary in Williamsburg, Virginia; Carlo Bellini, professor of modern languages

49. Pope Pius VI, who created the Diocese of Baltimore on April 6, 1789

50. Guy Lombardo

51. The Hill

52. The Astoria section of New York City

53. Teddy Roosevelt went to barber Thomas Zannetti, who lived in St. Albans, Queens.

54. Naples

55. 1950

56. Al Smith, whose father was born in Genoa

57. The Garibaldi Guard

58. 1601 Fuller Street NW

59. Dominic R. Massaro of New York City

60. Vince DiMaggio played for the Pittsburgh Pirates.

61. Santini

62. The Grucci Company, of Long Island, New York

63. Joseph J. DiCicco

64. Henry F. Viscardi, internationally known rehabilitator of the physically handicapped

65. Rosemary Dattolico Breslin

66. John N. LaCorte, founder of the Italian Historical Society of America

67. Marymount, in New York City

68. Camillo J. D'Urso

69. Antonio Meucci

70. Frank L. Rizzo

71. Joseph Petrosino, in 1883

72. Danny DiVito, of Asbury Park, New Jersey

73. Eddie Giacomin, with 49, 266 and 8 respectively

74. April 18, 1951

75. Parma

76. March 6, 1908

77. Constantino Brumidi (1880)

78. 1893 on Catherine Street in New York City

79. Francesco Vigo

80. 1920

81. Boating

82. Peter Lemengello

83. Charles DeLeo

84. The late Joe Gelardi

85. In 1984—it was a Christmas stamp designed by eight-year-old Daniel LaBoccetta of Richmond Hill, Queens.

86. Dan Floria, who died in 1965

87. Mrs. Gemma LaGuardia Gluck

88. Cesare Sabelli in 1928 from the seaplane *Roma*

89. Yes, in the 1960s, though most people knew him as Dennis James

90. Fairleigh Dickinson, in 1942

91. Rudy Vallee and Judge Salvatore A. Cotillo

92. Alfred A. Lama—the bill became the Mitchell-Lama Law.

93. Harvard University, by Robert Sprung

94. They were miners in Colorado.

95. 10 to 12 percent—of these, one hundred were awarded the Distinguished Service Cross.

96. They had permitted blacks to have equal status with whites in their shops.

97. Francis Cerbini, who was born in Italy in 1902 and emigrated to the United States in 1921

98. In the Ozone Park area

99. In 1977 in Elmwood Park, Illinois

100. Chet Forte (producer-director of ABC Sports), Linda Frattianne (1980 Olympic figure-skating medalist), Nick Buoniconti (star linebacker for the Miami Dolphins), Carmen Salvino (champion bowler) and Carl Furillo (outfielder with the old Brooklyn Dodgers baseball team)

101. the process of making paper from wood

102. Father Peter Rinaldi, S.D.B., who has written several books and dozens of articles on the subject

103. Father James E. Groppi (1931-1985)

104. The Browning Institute, headquartered in New York City

105. Dr. Anne Paolucci of St. John's University in New York City

106. Dr. Peter Sammartino, president emeritus of Fairleigh Dickinson University in New Jersey

107. This non-profit educational foundation was founded in 1985 to promote projects and special events connected with the Columbus quin-centennial celebration.

108. In the Botto House in Haledon, New Jersey, which in 1913 served as a headquarters for labor leaders during the historic Patterson Silk Strike

109. St. Ambrose

110. To honor a native son, Lt. Col. Frank Adamo, M.D., who discovered during World War II a revolutionary method to treat gangerene. He was also a prisoner of the Japanese during part of the war.

111. The Church of San Carlo al Corso

112. Saint Vincent Pallotti (1795-1850)

113. Foster Furcolo

114. *Attenzione*

115. Vincent Impellitteri

116. Ferdinand Pecora and Edward Corsi

117. At the time of his retirement in 1956, he was the only undefeated heavyweight champion in ring history.

118. Brockton, Massachusetts, in 1924.

119. Gene Caggiano and Al Colombo

120. After he knocked out Joe Louis in 1951

121. Paolo Soleri

122. Antonia Uccello

123. New Jersey

124. "But they left the subway"—an allusion to the fact that Italians were the largest group of laborers working on subway systems such as New York's

125. Three hundred

126. Nicola Sacco, in the Sacco-Vanzetti trial in 1921

127. He declared August 23, 1977, Nicola Sacco and Bartolomeo Vanzetti Memorial Day, stating that earlier "the conduct of many officials involved in the case sheds serious doubts on their willingness and ability to conduct the prosecution and trial fairly."

128. He was a former world flyweight champion.

129. John Basilone

130. Congressman Peter Rodino

131. Judge John Sirica

132. New Mexico

133. Illinois

134. President Jimmy Carter, in 1977

135. A fullback for the Los Angeles Rams from 1974 to 1976

136. The New York Cosmos

137. Dr. Rocco Petrone

138. Pioneer banker Amadeo P. Giannini (1870-1949)

139. Philip Mazzei

140. Patricia Beemer, in 1983

141. Michael Sisca. The magazine was founded in 1892.

142. On March 24, 1965, as she marched from Selma to Montgomery, Alabama

143. Captain Giovanni Dominis, who by this act introduced the salted salmon trade between the West and the East coasts of the country

144. In Canada, in 1902

145. Venice

146. Vincent Burnelli

147. Steve Florio

148. The Columbus Press

149. Dante Magnani

150. Daphne and Lamberth, Alabama

151. Peter Nichols

152. Amin A. deTarrazi

153. *The Italian Times,* which began operation in 1980

154. Joseph L. Andreis

155. In 1940, in New York City

156. George Coyne, S.J.

157. Senator John Orlando Pastore, elected in 1950

158. Bayonne, New Jersey

159. Guglielmo Marconi

Ye who love a nation's legends
Love the ballads of a people
That like voices from afar off
Call to us to pause and listen.

Longfellow

Visions of Italy

1. What is the original name of this painting by the late-nineteenth-century Italian artist Roberto Ferruzzi, now known as *The Madonna of the Street?*

reprinted from *Images*, published by the Center for Migration Studies

2. Who is this woman?

reprinted from *Images*, published by the Center for Migration Studies

3. This man founded a religious order specifically for the assistance of Italian immigrants. In 1901 he visited the United States and met with President Theodore Roosevelt to discuss the problems facing Italian immigrants in this country. Who is he?

courtesy ENIT

4. The most famous Italian colosseum is in Rome; however, this structure is in a city farther north. Name the location, better known as the home of two famous lovers.

courtesy ENIT

5. This tower in Siena was the home of St. Catherine, a famous fourteenth-century saint. Can you name it?

courtesy ENIT

6. Name this hilltop town. Need a hint? Raphael was born here in 1483.

courtesy the Italian Cultural Institute

7. Name this city in Tuscany which is considered to be one of the most remarkably preserved of all medieval hill towns.

courtesy ENIT

8. Italy has other leaning towers besides the famous one in Pisa. Name the city where this set of double leaning towers is found.

courtesy the Italian Cultural Institute

9. This literary giant wrote a historical novel which critics have ranked among the best ever written. Who is he, and what is his novel?

courtesy the Italian Cultural Institute

10. This woman was considered to be the greatest Italian actress—and by most critics the best actress in the world—in her time. She was born in Italy in 1859 and she died in the United States in 1924. Who was she?

courtesy *The Anthonium*

11. He is shown here as a medical corps sergeant and chaplain in the Italian army in World War I. In 1919, he wrote in his diary, "Either I achieve something with my life, or I bear a terrible responsiblity for wasting the Lord's mercies." Who did this man, then known as Father Roncalli, become?

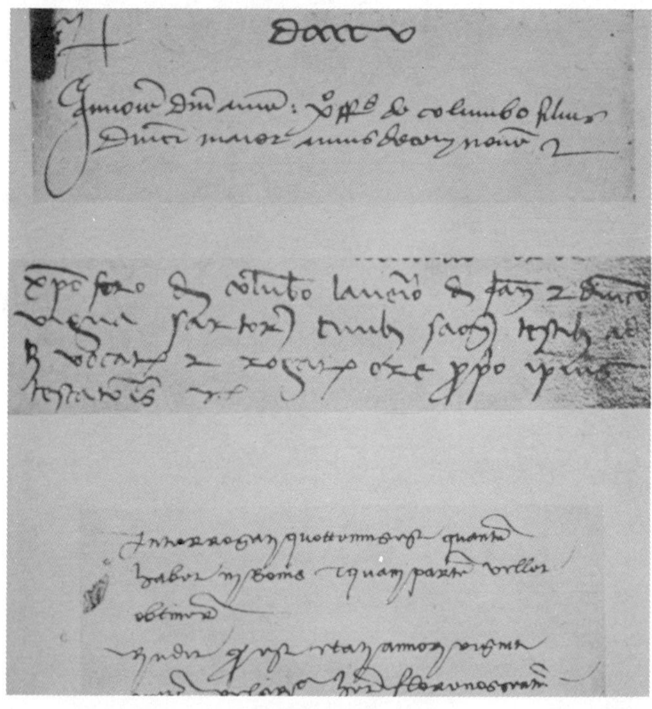

12. What historical value do these three document portions have?

13. From 1908 to 1935 this man was the general manager of what great opera house?

14. This Sicilian-born director was responsible for such films as *You Can't Take It With You* and *It's a Wonderful Life.* Who is he?

15. This man was called "the Michelangelo of the U.S. Capitol." Who was he?

16. This historical cathedral still stands in a mid-western city. Name the city and the Italian root of the building.

17. Besides the Vatican, there is yet another tiny state within the borders of Italy. It is the oldest and smallest republic in the world. Can you recognize it from this sixteenth-century print?

18. What is the subject (and title) of this Michelangelo fresco?

19. These are exterior and interior views of a part of the Vatican built decades ago. What purpose does the structure serve?

20. This man wrote the first book on the American Revolution to be published in Europe. Name him and the place of publication.

21. In this photograph an opera is being performed using the backdrop of the ancient pyramids in Egypt for authenticity. What opera is taking place?

22. This Italian composer based an opera on an actual occurence which took place in a court in Potenza. The opera is an all-time favorite. Who is its composer?

reprinted from *Images*, published by the Center for Migration Studies

23. This 1920s American screen idol was born in Castellaneta, Italy. Who was he?

reprinted from *Images*, published by the Center for Migration Studies

24. A photograph, circa 1950, of President Dwight D. Eisenhower accompanied by two sports greats to the annual Congressional baseball game in Washington, D.C. Who are the men to the President's left and right?

reprinted from *Images*, published by the Center for Migration Studies

25. In the course of this man's career, he served as defense counsel in the Sacco and Vanzetti case and presided at the International Military Trials of War Crimes at Nurenberg. He died in 1968. Who was he?

reprinted from *Images*, published by the Center for Migration Studies

26. A 1958 photograph of Anne Italiano in her old neighborhood, the Bronx—by what name is she now better known?

reprinted from *Images*, published by the Center for Migration Studies

27. This police officer startled the nation with his testimony before the Knapp Commission on police department corruption in New York in 1971. Al Pacino starred in the film version of his saga. Who is he?

reprinted from *Images*, published by the Center for Migration Studies

28. Father and son accepted four Academy Awards for their contributions to the 1975 film *The Godfather, Part II.* Who are they?

29. Name this church in Florence which is considered one of Italy's most perfect examples of Gothic architecture.

Answers

1. *Madonnina,* or "Little Madonna." The model for the painting was fourteen-year-old Angelina Cian, who was caring for her little brother in the hills near Padua when she was spotted by Ferruzzi. He never intended the painting to be of the Virgin Mary but titled it so because of the model's youth.

2. The first U.S. citizen to be canonized—Mother Cabrini

3. Bishop John Baptist Scalabrini (1839-1905), founder of the Congregation of the Missionaries of St. Charles. Today, "Scalabrinians" can be found in twenty countries in North and South America,

Europe and Australia, assisting all migrants and refugees.

4. Verona, home of Romeo and Juliet

5. The Mangia Tower

6. Urbino

7. San Gimignano

8. Bologna

9. Alessandro Manzoni (1785-1873), the author of *I Promessi Sposi* (1827)

10. Eleanora Duse, who never used make-up

11. Pope John XXIII (1881-1963)

12. They are all portions from official documents that prove Columbus was born in Genoa.

13. Giulio Gatti-Casazza headed the Metropolitan Opera house of New York during what critics called its "golden reign."

14. Frank Capra

15. Costantino Brumidi (1805-1880) earned the nickname because of the numerous frescos and paintings he did for that building.

16. This is the old cathedral of St. Louis, Missouri. It was built between 1831 and 1834 by Bishop Joseph Rosati (1789-1843), a native of Sora, near the city of Naples.

17. The Republic of San Marino

18. *The Last Judgment*

19. It houses the Vatican City's railroad station, which runs the shortest railway line in the world.

20. Carlo Botta, in Milan in 1808

21. Verdi's *Aida,* first produced in Cairo, Egypt, in 1871

22. Ruggiero Leoncavallo (1858-1919), composer of *I Pagliacci*

23. Rudolph Valentino

24. Joe DiMaggio of the New York Yankees on the left, heavyweight champ Rocky Marciano on the right

25. Judge Michael Angelo Musmanno, Pennsylvania State Supreme Court Justice

26. Anne Bancroft

27. Frank Serpico

28. Carmine Coppola (left) and Francis Ford Coppola

29. Santa Croce

Crossword puzzles are sometimes easy and sometimes a bit difficult. Readers of ITALIAN TRIVIA, nevertheless, are hereby invited to try their hands at the following puzzle, which we believe falls into the "easy" range. Remember, an Italian-American was one of the three who edited the first crossword book ever, an anthology from the *New York World,* published by Simon & Schuster on April 18, 1924. His name was Albert Prosper Buranelli, and he was assisted by F. Gregory Hartswich and Margaret Petheridge. So in honor of them all, let's give it a try!

Across

2. Initials of one of the greatest Florentine painters of the Renaissance usually known by his first name alone

5. Initials of a very famous order of Catholic preachers whose founder's name is one of the most popular among Italians

7. *Un amimale favorite*

8. Pat's full name in Italy

9. Initials of a seventeenth-century Neapolitan man who distinguished himself not only as a painter but as a writer of plays and satirical verses

10. Italian for "Savior": shortened form

11. Italian for "rare"

12. Italian for "king"

13. Initials of an 18th-century English architect who, returning to his homeland after four years in Italy, developed a decorative art style, Pompeiian in design, which soon displaced much of the English Chippendale style

14. Roman numeral nine

15. Italian for "here it is," or "behold"

Down

1. Italian for "male wolf"

2. Italian for "red"

3. Abbreviation for Senate and People of Rome (letters often found on ancient Roman coins)

4. Italian for "star" (also the name of a very famous twentieth-century Italian-American artist who first introduced the Futurism movement to America in 1913)

6. Italian for "Christmas"

7. Italian for "weigh" or "heavy"

13. First two letters of English translation of *reale*

Answers to Crossword Puzzle

Across

2. RS (Raphael Santi, 1483-1520)

5. OP (Standing for Order of Preachers or Dominicans; the popular name is Dominic.)

7. pet ("a favorite animal")

8. Pasquale

9. SR (Salvatore Rosa, 1615-1673)

10. Sal

11. *raro*

12. *re*

13. RA (Robert Adam, 1728-1792)

14. IX

15. Ecco

Down

1. *lupo*

2. *rosso*

3. *SPQR*

4. *stella* (The artist was Joseph Stella.)

6. *Natale*

7. *peso*

13. RO ("royal")

Nicholas Falco, a native New Yorker, was educated at City College of New York and St. John's University in Jamaica, New York, from which institution he received a Master of Library Science degree in 1965. He credits his parents with fostering in him a love for Italian and Italian-American history, and he has fond memories of growing up in the East Harlem and Bronx sections of the city hearing lively discussions of Italian politics, current events, literature, theater and the best way of making Italian sauce for pasta.

In the sixties and seventies, Falco was a contributing editor and then editor of the monthly paper *The Italo-American Times,* published in the Bronx. He has written a number of articles on local history for various magazines as well as edited *They Were Here,* a book recently issued by the Bronx Society of Science and Letters listing the contributions of past and present residents of the Bronx. Work with both the New York Public Library System and the Queens Borough Public Library in their archives and local history departments has led to lectures on local history, geneology and the problems in administering historical collections.

Falco is a member of the American Italian Historical Association, the Forum of Italian-American Educators, the National Italian American Foundation, the Italian Historical Society of America, the Catholic Library Association, the Society of American Archivists and the America-Italy Society. He and his wife Rose, who shares his enthusiasm for Italian-American culture, have traveled extensively throughout Italy and many Italian-American sections of American cities.